stress into
strength

Nick Arnett

stress into
strength

resilience routines for warriors,
wimps, and everyone in between

HARPERCOLLINS
LEADERSHIP

AN IMPRINT OF HARPERCOLLINS

Published by HarperCollins Leadership, an imprint of HarperCollins
Focus LLC.

Any internet addresses, phone numbers, or company or product
information printed in this book are offered as a resource and
are not intended in any way to be or to imply an endorsement by
HarperCollins Leadership, nor does HarperCollins Leadership
vouch for the existence, content, or services of these sites, phone
numbers, companies, or products beyond the life of this book.

ISBN 978-1-4002-2473-9 (eBook)
ISBN 978-1-4002-2469-2 (PBK)

Library of Congress Control Number: 2021937287

Printed in the United States of America
21 22 23 24 25 LSC 10 9 8 7 6 5 4 3 2 1

dedication

This book is dedicated to all of those who give their lives for others, figuratively or literally. Those who serve—paid or volunteer, private or public, religious or secular—to keep our society functioning.

I especially remember friends and family that we lost too soon: my brother John, who lost his life to bile duct cancer on December 28, 2020, my sister Susie, who lost her fight with ovarian cancer on May 9, 2020; my sister Lesley, who died in the H1N1 pandemic of 2009–10; John Heidish of Penn Hills Fire; Wesley Canning of the United States Marine Corps; and Jimmy McCluskey of Santa Clara County Fire.

contents

introduction:
stress, essential to life

When a coach or physical therapist urges you to work hard, that's because physical stress can become strength. Instead of "I should get more exercise despite the stress," choose "The stress of exercise will make me stronger."

When author Brené Brown describes the benefits of vulnerability and transparency, that's because social stress can become strength. Instead of "I should show up and be more real with others despite the stress," choose "The stress of showing up and being real will make me stronger."

When the Bible or other holy writing says, "Adversity builds character," that's because spiritual[1] stress can become strength. Instead of "I should take on new challenges despite the stress," choose "The stress of adversity will make me stronger."

E very two to three days, I escape the suburbia of Silicon Valley for a trail, strap a heavy pack on my back, set my phone to track my progress, and hike three or four miles, occasionally more. I hike fast. On a flat trail, it takes me about forty-two minutes to cover three miles. That speed is significant because to qualify for wildland fire assignments, one of my part-time jobs, each spring I have to pass the "pack test"—three miles in forty-five minutes or less, carrying forty-five pounds. It is on level ground, but no running is allowed.[2]

For a guy who is eligible for Social Security, those workouts are *stressful*. My heart rate reaches about 160 beats per minute, I sweat a lot, sometimes I feel nauseated, and frequently I'd like to just quit.

When I hit the trail with that heavy pack, my automatic stress response activates. My body releases stress hormones, giving me energy, focus, and stamina. You've probably heard the stress reaction called "fight or flight," a name that certainly describes what I'm doing. Physical stress turns into physical strength, endurance, and resilience when we do it at the right intervals and also activate our physical renewal response. This was dubbed "rest and digest" by the same scientist who coined fight or flight. Resting and digesting heals the damage done by physical stress and triggers growth.

The right kinds and amounts of fight or flight and rest and digest, at the right intervals, make us *physically* stronger and more resilient. Thanks to regular physical challenges, rest, and nutrition, I am now faster, stronger, and need less rest to bounce back from intense effort.

Fight or flight and rest and digest describe physical reactions and renewal, but stress is also mental and spiritual. Training for the pack test is mentally stressful: I need to stay focused. Distracting thoughts and feelings will slow me down. If I pull out my phone and start reading messages, the app that tracks my speed quickly reflects that distraction.

Sometimes I get in "the zone" (a "flow state" that I'll describe further), and it feels like I'm floating down the trail. But more often the pack makes my shoulders ache and makes every step a chore. The mental stress includes acknowledging and setting aside the desire to turn away from the discomfort and occasional pain. I remind myself that fatigue is an emotion that we feel long before we are really out of energy. Although it is critical to know how hard we can push ourselves, there's no safe way to know without training.

The temptation to compare myself to others is also mentally stressful. When I work with a crew that is younger (and they pretty much all are) and I'm falling behind, I remind myself that what other people think of me is none of my business.

"Defend and distance" is my name for our social stress response. It is mental fight or flight, the urge to explain away or avoid uncomfortable feelings, embarrassment, and judgment. On the trail, that's coming from within me, but its roots lie in my relationships with others. I learned those voices and the language to describe them from my parents, teachers, and other influential people.

Just as we recover from fight or flight by activating rest and digest, we have a social renewal activator: "tend and befriend." When researchers discovered it about twenty years ago, they labeled it a stress response, but it clearly is more about renewal. Tending and befriending repairs damage done by defensive and distancing thoughts and behavior and turns social stress into strength to think more clearly, manage emotions, and bond with others.

The right kinds and amounts of defend and distance and tend and befriend, at the right intervals, make us stronger and more resilient. Thanks to regular social challenges and support, I am stronger mentally and emotionally.

The spiritual stress of my workouts is a struggle with goals and priorities. I joke sometimes at fires, when I'm exhausted from climbing a steep hill with heavy gear: "I'm questioning my life choices right now." Why am I doing this? The answer is complicated. It's partly because of Silicon Valley's ageism—good job offers are scarce for product managers, my former career, over fifty. It is also because about seven years ago I began doing peer support and crisis intervention for public safety agencies, including California's state fire department, Cal Fire, at large fires. I want to have a better idea of the work they do (and not just the glamorous parts).

Staying motivated is often difficult. Sometimes I'll remind my-self that I'll need the energy on the next fire. Younger people are usually leading, and it's often all I can do to keep up with the slower ones. I also stay motivated by reminding myself that exercise does more good at my age than any other time of life. I'll recall my doctor joking that he wishes he had my lab test results (which weren't always quite so good—a few years ago I was on the borderline of type 2 diabetes). I also do it because every little boy wants to be a firefighter and there's still some little boy inside me. I was a paramedic in my twenties, but it wasn't the same. Decades later, any day I get to ride in a fire engine—or even better, to *drive* one—is a very cool day.

Working at a job I know I will never excel at (in the physical aspects, anyway) also forces me to struggle with the feeling that nothing I do is ever good enough. Following orders in a paramilitary organization, especially when I'm just another body on the line, is another struggle for me. I'm forced to learn to admit "I don't know" much more often than I'd like. But on a fire, getting in over your head can be deadly. I also do it *because* it is hard. "Embrace the suck," a military motto, is also dear to many wildland firefighters. (But the idea goes back at least as far as Shakespeare's *Henry VI*: "Let thee embrace me, sour adversity, for wise men say it is the wisest course.")

Looking back, I realize that even though I didn't know it, another "why" was so that I could write this book, even though I don't talk a lot about firefighting in it. And yes, I also do it to pay rent and put food on the table.

I call our spiritual stress reaction "selfish and survivalist" because, under stress, our perspective and priorities narrow; we become concerned mostly about ourselves and those closest to us. But living that way all the time, like being stuck in fight or flight or defend and distance, will wear you down. I call the renewal activator "pause and plan" because we need to periodically restore our perspective and to acknowledge and revisit our goals and priorities so that we can adapt them to current circumstances.

stress reactions as gifts

Whether you are a firefighter, teacher, plumber, or Hollywood star, life can be hard, challenging, sometimes overwhelming. That's normal. You will feel stress, even on ordinary days. That's more than just okay: the gift of your stress reactions is to allow you to respond *flexibly* to your circumstances.[3] Your body, mind, and spirit can quickly, sometimes instantly, switch gears to seize opportunities, overcome challenges, and cope with threats. The more flexible and resilient you are, the less sticky your stress reactions become. The damaging effects of stress go away and benefits accrue if you quickly return to calm when your situation no longer calls for the speedy reflexes, focus, energy, and stamina your stress reactions give you.

This book is for warriors, wimps, and everyone in between because we are all in between. We are never just one thing. As warriors we fight against what is wrong. As leaders we stand up for what is right. As peacemakers we bring unity. As reformers we divide and drive change. We are consumers who trade money for goods and services, and we are producers who create goods and services for money. We are helpless and helpful, perfectionists and failures, performers and audience, responsible and carefree, thoughtful and impulsive, dominating and vulnerable.

Our stress reactions help us perform. People who feel some stress when tackling a challenging task perform better than those who say they are completely relaxed. Researchers measuring stress-hormone levels found that students and paratroopers perform better when stress-hormone levels rise.[4]

Let me be clear about what this book teaches: to be fully *alive* means to embrace your stress reactions as gifts. You don't need protection from stress any more than you need protection from working out at the gym, from being transparent and vulnerable with friends, or from the struggle to balance care for yourself and others. Your stress reactions help you to live and live well. Without *some* stress, no living creature would ever adapt, develop, or grow. Together, our stress and renewal reactions make us grow and stay strong, healthy, flexible, and resilient. Shunning stress is a path to weakness, disease, boredom, and unhappiness.

Multiple research studies support the fundamental idea behind this book: stress that is *moderate and intermittent* is the path to greater resilience.[5] Too little or too much adversity is not good; we become strongest somewhere in the middle. Even childhood trauma, associated with a wide range of long-term physical and psychological ailments, can strengthen victims of physical (but not commonly for emotional) neglect and abuse.[6] Resilience, once believed available only to a handful of lucky people, can arise from everyday stress and renewal. It is "ordinary magic," in the words of psychologist Ann Masten, whose work focuses on resilience in children and adolescents.[7]

Before going further, a caution. Although stress can become strength, that doesn't make it okay to inflict or, worse, to "prescribe" trauma, or pain for others. Habits of regular stress and renewal, tailored to your gifts and challenges, will strengthen you. That means regularly getting out of your comfort zone, physically, socially, and spiritually. But only *you* can know the boundaries of your comfort zone; only *you* can know all of the stressors you are experiencing; only *you* can know how much renewal you need and are getting. Although life deals us unchosen stressors and opportunities for renewal, each of us has the exclusive ability and right to select and control the additional kinds, amounts, and rhythms of stress and renewal that we believe will benefit us. Even when you are a parent, leader, teacher, coach, or other kind of mentor who challenges others to help them reach their potential, you often cannot see when you cross the line from helping to hurting.

Under stress, we often instinctively go it alone. Fighting, fleeing, defending, distancing, selfishness, and survivalist strategies, while helpful in the short run, isolate us. Renewal can restore the connections we abandon during stress; and this is essential because remaining disconnected is unhealthy. Yet connections also break for reasons outside of our control; some losses are permanent. People die. Although faith may tell us they live on, our senses still feel the loss. Renewal can also mean connecting in entirely new ways after loss, betrayal, abandonment, or any other change.

Reading this book can help you become more resilient. But if only your thinking changes, the book will have little impact. I have done my best to follow my literary agent's and publisher's repeated instructions to stay practical and not too intellectual. I hope I have succeeded, because even though resilience needs your mind, it isn't the best place to begin. Your body and heart matter a great deal. "The longest journey you will make in life is from your head to your heart," a quote attributed to various people, contains great truth about starting points for change. Our bodies, not just our minds, store stress and trauma.

Feeling stress means you *care*; people do not react to things they don't care about. The idea that all stress is bad for you is dangerous; living in fear of stress will hurt you. We *need* stress— the right kinds of physical, social, and spiritual stress and renewal, in the right amounts, at the right intervals—to grow and to stay strong and flexible. Stress can transform us physically and mentally, often for the better. We naturally tend to focus on the negatives of traumatic stress, even though few people end up with lasting negative effects. Many respond by becoming more resilient—building their social support, increasing their self-confidence, and improving their coping skills.[8] Without overcoming adversity, you cannot know, really *know* in your gut, your true capabilities.

Stress was given its bad reputation in part from a famous (and cruel) experiment on dogs in the 1960s, which showed that repeated, inescapable electric shocks can lead to "learned helplessness." The dogs seemed to give up, refusing to even try when the shocks became controllable.[9] The study became an explanation of how stress leads to depression and other mental health issues. More recent research shows that, rather than learning helplessness, the dogs were actually failing to learn control. That distinction is not nearly as significant as an often-overlooked part of the original research: learned helplessness *disappeared* when the researchers increased the time interval between shocks. In other words, giving the dogs time for sufficient *renewal* erased the negative effects.[10] Timing is everything. Stress marathons are bad. Stressful sprints can strengthen us.

Regular, well-timed renewal is the key to turning stress into strength, but renewal is more than just getting away from sources of stress. Automatic, sticky stress reactions don't necessarily quiet just because you get away—you may still be in the flight part of fight or flight. Renewal activation, not so automatic, needs to be intentional.

Renewal—pausing, resting, nourishing, taking care of yourself and others—repairs, restores, builds, and maintains physical, mental, and spiritual strength and flexibility. The right rhythms of stress and renewal can rewire your brain and reshape your body. This book's goal is to help you discover and nurture natural, life-, and health-giving patterns of stress and renewal that your body, mind, and spirit need.

Modern authors often describe stress reactions as unfortunate, troublesome leftovers from prehistory. The story goes something like this: Ancient humans, in frequent danger from predators and other dangers, developed a fight-or-flight reaction to help escape from or do battle with lions, tigers, and so on. In the modern world, the story concludes, we no longer face such dangers, yet the stress reactions still happen and will slowly kill us.

Although we do live in a remarkably different environment than most of our ancestors, little of this account is relevant. Seeing stress as a problem or disease is understandable from the viewpoint of therapists who daily face the negative consequences of trauma. Violence, accidents, and natural disasters still happen. Our stress reactions help us respond to them, and to learn from them, so that we might cope better next time. In other words, we have a built-in drive to learn from negative experiences—to expand our tool kits, becoming more flexible—in hope that we (and those we teach) will respond better to similar ones in the future.

putting stress in its place

> Good judgment is the result of experience and experience is
> the result of bad judgment.
>
> —ANONYMOUS

When psychologists promote resilience, they often talk about building "protective factors." In that context, stress is still a bogeyman that needs to be warded off. But not all stress is traumatic, and we react to more than just threats to our survival. Although the modern world is *physically* safer than much of the past, other kinds of challenging and threatening opportunities and risks have increased. We depend far more than our uncivilized ancestors on our ability to navigate complex social systems and to adhere to modern codes of ethics.

Living in the modern world calls for sophisticated social skills, which give us the ability to read others' emotions and regulate our own, enabling the alliances and other structures through which people cooperate and compete to accomplish far, far more than individuals or simpler tribes ever could. We also have a greater need for spiritual skills, to see a much bigger picture than our ancestors, sorting through complex, competing priorities and to adopt values such as reverence for life, liberty, and equality, which are the moral and ethical foundations of modern civilizations.[11]

Even though we are far from perfect at these social and spiritual skills, without them we would be powerless in the modern world. Our astonishing ability to form organizations and networks to solve problems or accomplish tasks with teamwork, and our agreement on fairness, and right versus wrong, have made us the dominant species on the planet. To be human means to care and therefore feel stress about relationships and values. Looking at that stress as a problem is self-defeating: stress about the things we care about drives us to learn and improve. Think of feeling stress as a signal: "this is important."

For example, embarrassment is one of the most potent human social emotions. Although higher animals have social lives, few scientists argue that they feel the stress of embarrassment the way we do. Animals' social connections are far simpler than ours, typically little more than a hierarchy of dominance. The threat of embarrassment can drive us to be effective team players. Animals don't feel stress about fair play because they don't care about it. Similarly, guilt and shame are spiritual stressors, unknown to animals but essential signals for regulating modern human behavior.

Let's put stress in its proper place. Living things sing complex melodies of stress and renewal, orchestrated by interactions of internal, biological clocks and external events. When we rise to challenges, ward off threats, or seize opportunities, those are the *notes,* varying in intensity and quality. We easily mistake the notes for the melody, but without rhythm and rests, notes are noise, tiresome and exhausting. The "rests" in life's melodies are the downtime when we renew, through calming reconnection with ourselves and nature, connecting with others to help process thoughts and feelings, and when doors swing open to growth, creativity, and inspirations that give life meaning. Renewal turns stress into strength.

Stress gets far more attention than renewal, but that is unsurprising. Our brains have a "negative bias," which you will read more about later: our natural tendency to focus on and react more to negatives than positives. Warnings about negative effects of stress are attention grabbers because they shout, "Danger!" Meanwhile, the positive effects of renewal reactions and hormones, the neurophysiological systems that turn stress into strength, get far less attention than they deserve.

I'm using *renewal,* rather than the typical word, *recovery,* because recovery is defined as "a return to a normal state of health, mind, or strength," which would imply that having a stress reaction is abnormal. It is not. At the gym, on the job, or in your living room, there is nothing unhealthy about your brain and body revving up to cope. In fact, those who strive, take on challenges, and seize opportunities are healthier and happier than people who try to avoid stress. Excessive or unrelenting stress is bad, but jumping to the conclusion that "easy" is the path to satisfaction or happiness is incorrect. Easy cannot make you stronger. Easy cannot give you a sense of accomplishment.

I hope it is becoming clear that when I talk about developing "strength" in this book, it is not just about gaining control. The kind of strength I'm talking about is *empowering*; it increases your sense of autonomy and influence. My hope is to give some hints about how to have a better life, beyond minimizing distress and maximizing pleasure. Well-being is a better description. People generally agree on the definitions of physical and mental health, but spiritual health is another story. In these pages, it means being fully alive, engaged, connected, and vital, placing value on finding or creating meaning in life's trials and joys rather than seeking only to satisfy self-centered desires and cravings. I set aside arguments about whether altruism truly exists; as social creatures, we are interdependent individuals, wired so that when we help others, we help ourselves.

We sometimes talk about ourselves as if we were machines: "I need to refuel" is a common expression. Don't think of yourself as a machine; stress only wears them down. You are not like that, not at all. After ordinary stress (and often after trauma), if you get the right kind of rest and nourishment (more than just sleep, food, and water), neurochemical signals travel throughout your mind and body, quieting your stress response while announcing that it is time for your mind and body to shift into renewal. Machines will never do that, no matter how much "exercise" and "rest" you give them. Life is astonishing compared to machines: we can increase our horsepower through well-timed stress and renewal.

Living things don't just heal and grow; they also adapt. Despite the software domain called "machine learning," ordinary machines are incapable of learning to adapt to a changing environment. No matter how often you drive your car off road, it will never invent four-wheel drive. People who experienced stress—

an opportunity and challenge—when confronted with impassable territory, responded by inventing four-wheel drive. Stress not only tells us that we need to learn and grow, it brings about changes in our bodies and minds to help us do so—especially when we also experience renewal. For example, we remember things better under moderate stress, but those memories are fixed in place during the renewal of sleep.

We also misunderstand the nature of stress and renewal when we treat the complexity of life as nothing more than a collection of feedback loops. The response of living systems to change is far more difficult to predict than simple feedback. Our complex, self-regulating systems are full of surprises, such as thresholds that trigger dramatic changes. For example, the stress hormone adrenaline causes your heart to beat faster and your blood vessels to expand—up to a point. When your adrenaline level rises high enough to cross the "beta" threshold, your blood vessels *constrict,* and so your blood pressure rises.[12] In complex ways, living systems *learn* from and adapt to the environment. For example, for better or worse, reducing or increasing stimulation will alter your stress and renewal systems.

None of this means that stress can't hurt you. Too much stress without enough renewal will wear you down. Too little stress will weaken you. Even the wrong *pattern* of stress and renewal can hurt you. As any athlete can tell you, the trick to avoiding injury while building and keeping physical strength is to find the right methods and rhythms of the right kinds and amounts of exercise, rest, and nourishment. The same principle applies to building mental strength for thinking and managing emotions, and to building spiritual strength of character—your values, mission, and purpose.

Health is not just the absence of illness or injury. A healthy life looks like a series of sprints, rather than a marathon of unending work and stress. The right intervals of the right kinds of rest and nourishment between sprints will enable you to seize bigger opportunities, take on greater challenges, and cope better with difficulties. Even when something looks like a marathon for society, such as the unfolding COVID-19 pandemic, we perform at our best *individually* by alternating sprints with rest and nourishment in the right rhythms. Feeling guilty about your downtime, your renewal time, is self-sabotage.

Avoiding stress on principle is a mistake. Instead, consider asking yourself, "Will this give me more energy than it takes?" (Question coined by Janet Childs, director of the Bay Area CISM Team.) If so, embrace it. If not, skip or postpone it. Your answer may change depending on what is going on in your life. For example, putting up holiday decorations may be an energy giver most years, but if you are in grief, it is likely to take more energy than it gives you. "Maybe next year," would be a healthy decision.

reframing your stress

All the commercials on TV today are for antidepressants, for Prozac or Paxil. And they get you right away. "Are you sad? Do you get stressed, do you have anxiety?" "Yes, I have all those things! I'm alive!"

—ELLEN DEGENERES

When you feel stress, remind yourself that it helps you to seize opportunities, rise to challenges, and answer threats. Psychologists call this "positive reframing," and it helps keep your stress autopilot[13] from overreacting. To help you accept the idea that stress can be good for you, consider what you would think of a teacher or coach who never pushed you out of your comfort zone. Feeling stress means you *care*, because we only feel stress about things we care about—and caring makes you stronger.

Ask a physical therapist how to heal or a weightlifter how to build muscles and their answers would go like this:

- Establish safety.
- Choose weights and movements a bit beyond your comfort zone.
- As you work out, pay attention to your technique, reactions, and long-term progress.
- Wait the right amount of time between sets and between workouts.
- Get enough rest and nutrition between workouts.
- Remember why you are exercising and the good it's doing.
- When you don't keep to your schedule, start over.

Weightlifting is stressful—and not just physically. Like all exercise, it also requires mental energy to focus and spiritual energy to stay motivated. Despite, or more correctly *because* of the stress, if you practice regularly and safely, and get rest and nutrition, you can develop and keep your strength. Getting out of your comfort zone in the weight room causes small injuries—"micro tears"—to your muscles. Rather than being bad for you, these are *essential* to increasing your strength.

Ordinary stress becomes harmful only if one of the elements isn't right—safety, intensity, technique, attention, intervals, nourishment, purpose, and unlimited permission to fail and start over.

Even though we sometimes talk about "good" and "bad" stress, which psychologists call "eustress" and "distress," our reactions hardly differ. Imagine scientists are remotely measuring your heart rate, respirations, muscle tension, sweat, hormone levels, brain activity, and so forth. For most of life's ordinary trials, challenges, and celebrations (positive events also make our hearts beat faster), "eustress" and "distress" will look the same. You might be lifting weights, but it could be that your boss is criticizing you. You might have tripped and fallen, enjoyed the thrill of a roller coaster, felt embarrassed, gotten married, won the lottery, had a fender bender, had stage fright, were in awe of the beauty of a sunrise, or you are nervously watching your favorite sports team in a close playoff game. Unless you feel truly threatened, helpless, or overwhelmed, your "good" and "bad" stress reactions look the same.

Research into "posttraumatic growth" shows that with sufficient renewal you can even transform psychological injuries into new strength—but no one is suggesting that it doesn't leave scars. Healing and growth do not guarantee that you won't still feel distress sometimes about past difficulties.

Even though activating renewal can calm your stress reactions, your stress and renewal systems aren't like the opposite ends of a seesaw. They can be active at the same time, giving you peak performance—a "flow state," sometimes called being "in the zone," in which you lose yourself in a challenging, even painful, task that feels almost effortless and enormously satisfying. Getting into a flow state doesn't happen by accident. It becomes more likely when you regularly practice activating your renewal reactions. For example, mental disciplines such as meditation and mindfulness contribute to reaching a flow state by bringing you into the present. Rituals, such as familiar, calming music, can prime your mind and body for flow. Perfectionism is an obstacle to flow.

In this book, I'll describe stress and renewal in the three dimensions I have already mentioned: physical, social, and spiritual. Remember that your stress reactions, far from being the liability implied by ideas such as "toxic stress," are gifts that allow you to rise to challenges, seize opportunities, and, yes, also to cope with threats. As you will read later, these gifts only become problems when you overuse them. I'll offer some tools to help you gain insight into how and when you are doing that.

- Think of your physical stress response (fight or flight) as changes to your body that help you rise to *material* challenges, opportunities, and threats—acquiring, enhancing, defending, owning, and using things, including your body, finances, tools, and other possessions. Physical stress becomes strength when you activate renewal by *resting and digesting*.

■ Your social stress response (defend or distance) changes the way you think and feel. It helps you rise to the mental and emotional challenges, opportunities, and threats of dealing with people: enemies, competitors, teachers, coaches, mentors, family, communities, tribes—living, working, competing, cooperating, and playing with others. Social stress becomes strength when you activate renewal by *tending and befriending*.[14]

■ Your spiritual stress response (selfish and survivalist) changes your values and perspective, leading you to focus more on immediate rather than long-term or big-picture concerns. It helps when you encounter challenges, opportunities, or threats to your priorities, urging you to focus more on yourself and those you care most about. Spiritual stress becomes strength when you activate renewal by *pausing and planning*.[15]

	Stress Response	Renewal Activation	Strength
Physical	Fight or Flight	Rest and Digest	Doing, Owning
Social	Defend or Distance	Tend and Befriend	Thinking, Feeling
Spiritual	Selfish or Survivalist	Pause and Plan	Purpose, Priorities

Although it is helpful to consider these dimensions of stress and renewal separately, they are not truly independent. Any type of stress reaction can rev you up and wear you down physically, mentally, and spiritually. Similarly, any kind of renewal can have physical, mental, and spiritual benefits.

Stress and renewal, *of the right kind, in the right amounts, and at the right intervals,* are the way that living things heal, grow, build strength, and become more resilient to bounce back from adversity. This is true for more than just muscles. It applies to your immune system, hormone levels, emotions, and thinking.

Only in the last few decades have psychologists begun to systematically research the idea that stress can lead to strength, under names such as "posttraumatic growth," "stress-related growth," and "adversarial growth." (This is no doubt due in part to the fact that the concept of psychological stress is very new, from the 1950s.) Yet the idea that difficulties can build strength, even leading to great transformation, has been a common theme in myth, literature, and religions for millennia. It also shows up in our language, in phrases such as "necessity is the mother of invention," "no pain, no gain," "use it or lose it," "adversity builds character," "pain is weakness leaving the body," "suffering is a grace," and "what doesn't kill you makes you stronger."

Whether stress is primarily physical, social, or spiritual, it affects us in all three dimensions. For stress to become strength, we need renewal in all three. You might assume that renewal is the result of getting what you need. But that's only half the story. *Giving*—in a spirit of generosity—is also renewing. The way in which you receive makes a difference also—gratefulness is renewing. In contrast, self-righteous giving (unwanted advice and criticism) and taking more than your fair share are counterproductive. When we open our hearts to gratefulness and generosity, we are tending and befriending, connecting as equals, rather than acting out the stress-driven, judgmental myth of self-sufficiency, which divides the world into haves and have-nots.

EXAMPLES: PHYSICAL STRESS INTO STRENGTH

◆ Periodically exposing yourself to the stress of high heat helps your body adapt, lessening the likelihood of heat exhaustion or stroke.

◆ Vaccines and low exposure to microbes can build protection by stressing your immune system, triggering production of antibodies that will protect you against later exposure.

◆ Although chronic stress without renewal weakens your immune system, the immediate effect of a stress reaction is to strengthen it.[16]

◆ The stress of intermittent fasting can help you lose weight, improve your health, and extend your life span—but timing is key, recent research shows.[17]

◆ Growing evidence shows that small doses of ionizing radiation, generally seen as harmful, could *reduce* cancer by "toughening" your cells.[18]

◆ Evidence is accumulating that daily drinking a few cups of coffee (a stimulant that activates stress reactions) reduces your risk of stroke, type 2 diabetes, and other ailments.[19]

◆ Low doses of sunlight build protection from cancers, including skin cancer. (But still use sunscreen!)[20]

◆ The stress of a cold shower provides some of the same benefits as intense exercise.

◆ Deep tissue massage hurts, but benefits have been documented in sports, cancer patients, premature infants, intensive care units, during labor and childbirth, and more.

◆ Calluses—strong skin—form only if you undergo the right rhythms of stress and renewal. For example, practicing guitar periodically and resting your fingertips makes it possible to play well without injury.

◆ Conifer forests cannot reproduce without the occasional stress of fire. In the western United States, decades of fire suppression—lack of stress—has weakened millions of trees, leaving them susceptible to beetles and catastrophic fires.

◆ High-intensity interval training (HIIT) is a pattern of alternating short bursts of intense exercise with rest or lower-intensity exercise. Research has shown that it improves health at a cellular level, making it one of the most efficient ways to increase your fitness, cardiovascular health, cholesterol, and blood sugar levels.[21]

◆ Evidence is growing that, despite health concerns about "free radicals," the irritation caused by small amounts of them in mitochondria (our cellular energy factories) is beneficial.[22] Naturally occurring antibacterials, antifungals, and antigrazing compounds—hot spices, tannins in wine, the smell of Brussels sprouts, and so forth—appear to help stop aging and make you stronger.

EXAMPLES: MENTAL STRESS INTO STRENGTH

Challenging thoughts or feelings can rewire your brain and improve stress and renewal-hormone levels.

◆ Learning can be tough, but it yields skills and knowledge that allow you to seize opportunities and cope with the intellectual and emotional challenges of using your mind. More than a century ago, psychologists named our increased memory and ability to learn under stress the Yerkes-Dodson Law,[23] which especially holds true for simpler learning and memory. Our "flashbulb memory" for details when we hear big news, especially if it is negative, is an example. Thus, most people who heard about the 9/11 attacks can tell you exactly where they were and what they were doing at the time. Note that *extreme* stress is helpful only for learning or remembering simple things; more difficult subjects are learned better and new habits are formed more easily under relatively mild stress.

◆ "Vulnerability is the birthplace of innovation, creativity, and change," writes researcher Brené Brown, author of *The Gifts of Imperfection* and other books on courage, vulnerability, shame, and empathy. Letting down your guard, "getting real" with partners, friends, therapists, and others can feel quite unsafe, yet it allows us to process stress and trauma, grow closer, and enjoy stronger relationships.

◆ Healthy expression of difficult feelings—venting—is often the only way to let them go. Although stressful, positive venting can be powerful for the person venting and those who hear it.[24] (This does not mean that *complaining* is good for you or anyone else.)

EXAMPLES: SPIRITUAL STRESS INTO STRENGTH

◆ Rituals, initiations, and rites of passage, whether religious or secular—marriage, funerals, graduations, retirement parties, coming-of-age events, and so forth—may be sources of anxiety or even injury, yet they are often regarded as essential, transformative, and foundational to a society's strength.

◆ Altruism, generosity, and caring for others—giving away your time, money, belongings—can stress your resources, yet research shows a strong connection between resilience and generosity.

> ◆ Meditation, mindfulness, yoga, martial arts, and other mind-body practices can be quite challenging yet have well-documented benefits.

Realize that the stress-into-strength formula is true for *all* living things, including pathogens. For example, a bacterium you are trying to get rid of might become worse if the antibiotic dose and intervals are right for strengthening it (and wrong for you)! That's why you are always instructed to take all of your antibiotics, on the prescribed schedule, even if you are feeling better.

myth busting

MYTH: TOXIC STRESS

Unfortunately, stress as disease is a common idea, even though you would be hard pressed to find it before the 1950s, when researchers first proposed it. Before then, the word *stress* was not applied to psychology. Now we know that much of the funding for those stress studies came from the tobacco industry, which was selling cigarettes as an antidote to stress. The industry also promoted the myth of "toxic stress" to cast doubt about tobacco's role in cancer and cardiovascular and other diseases.[25] The pioneering researcher Hans Selye had used a far more appropriate word—*strain*—initially. Selye eventually regretted that he used the word *stress* to mean both the cause and its effect, giving rise to the confusing idea that stress causes itself, which led him to coin the word *stressor* to describe sources of stress.[26]

It is understandable that clinical psychologists have focused on the negative effects of stress—it's what they see every day in their offices. That's like emergency room doctors, seeing only the results of unsafe exercise, concluding that physical activity is lethal, especially if they were unaware of its benefits or that most people, most of the time, are not injured when they work out.

In 2012, University of Wisconsin researchers dropped a bombshell on the idea of toxic stress. They did a big analysis to see who lived and who died among thirty thousand U.S. adults who had filled out a health questionnaire eight years earlier. As you might expect, people who said they believe that stress affects health, who also reported medium or high stress, were far more likely to have died. But people who said they did not believe that stress affects health lived the longest, even if they reported high stress![27]

Feeling stress is not the health hazard—fearing stress is.

Also, it was Big Tobacco that funded the cardiologists who came up with the idea of the "type A," high-stress, "killer" personality, which also has been debunked. Seeking challenges is healthy; negative emotions are not.

> Stress happens when something you care about is at stake. It's not a sign to run away—it's a sign to step forward.
>
> **—KELLY MCGONIGAL**

Another strong argument against toxic stress is that you can get relief from one kind of stress by replacing it with another stress, one more predictable and under your control. For example, intense and stressful physical exercise can help you recover from mental and emotional stress. Watching your favorite sports team in a close game is stressful but can provide a healing break, especially in the company of trusted friends.

It seems that Franklin D. Roosevelt had it right: "The only thing we have to fear is fear itself." Indeed, fear of stress will stop you from showing up for life. It leads you away from health, strength, and resilience. Sometimes we fall down, fail, or have our hearts broken, but there's nothing weak or "toxic" about those stresses, as long as you also get what you need to heal and grow. Resilience is about how you respond, not who you are—not how many times you fall down but how many times you get up, as the saying goes.

Ignoring the benefits of stress is yet another example of our negative bias, the tendency to focus on and react more strongly to risk and danger than to positives.

MYTH: "THAT'S TRAUMATIC"

When I teach crisis intervention, I emphasize that my students should never, ever assume that an experience was traumatic for the people involved. "There is no such thing as a traumatic incident," I say, which they often find confusing. "Never intervene based on *what happened*," I explain. "Look at how people are *reacting*."

People who go through the same high-stress event may react in different ways. One might go to bed that night, sleep well, and never be significantly affected or changed by the experience. Another might be traumatized and struggle to return to previous levels of functioning. That person might never be the same again.

How people react to an experience, whether they find it stressful or traumatic, has relatively little to do with what happened. Genes, how well you sleep, what kind of past experiences you have had, your social support, your beliefs, and, undoubtedly, other factors contribute to how you will react. Here is the great danger in assuming that an event was traumatic: if you are persuasive, you can *make* it traumatic. *You* can become the source of stress that pushes another person—or even *yourself*—from high stress into trauma.

Perception is powerful. The Wisconsin study showed perception's power to transform the effects of stress. Stress is inescapable for living things, so if you worry that stress is killing you, you have set yourself up for chronic rather than intermittent stress. Chronic stress will wear you down.

MYTH: STRESS IS ONLY ABOUT DANGER

You may have been taught to associate stress only with threats, but *opportunities and challenges* also provoke stress reactions. Your stress response is not just a leftover from the days humans lived "in the wild" with greater physical danger.

When your brain's stress autopilot activates, the intensity of your reaction depends on how much you care about the situation and how much immediate risk and control you *feel*. This is about your gut, not logic. If your autopilot feels confident that you can take control, you'll have a *challenge* reaction—excitement. If not, you'll have a *threat* reaction—anxiety that may also feel exciting. The more risk and less control you feel, the more it will feel like anxiety than excitement and the more your stress autopilot will drown out logical thinking, letting automatic reactions take over. Life-and-death situations will often provoke this, but so may less obvious situations, such as a chance for love or the potential of embarrassment. Seeing an opportunity will usually trigger a challenge, rather than threat reaction, since you can choose to walk away—until you commit yourself. Then you'll find out if your autopilot feels like you can cope!

MYTH: FEELING STRESS IS WEAKNESS

The world record for weightlifting is 1,067 pounds. You wouldn't call the record setter "weak" because he failed to lift 1,068! Yet we often talk and behave as if feeling *any* effect of stress, or any need for renewal, reveals weakness. Yes, everyone leaves the weight room tired, unable to lift as much as they could when they entered. But the next day, after resting, they may be even *stronger*. In other words, it is *normal* to temporarily feel weaker during and immediately after experiencing the benefits of stress, even though it is strengthening you in the long run.

I used to think that "trigger warnings" were a good idea. About a year after the 9/11 attacks, a friend sent me a digital slide show with a poem he had written, praising first responders. One of the photos showed people falling—jumping—to their deaths from the World Trade Center. I became angry.

"I wish he'd warned me about those pictures. I hate those pictures. I never want to see them again. He should have told me they were in there."

Dave, my friend and business partner, said, "I can see why that would really bother you."

Huh? I didn't know what he meant.

"That Easter fire on the South Side."

A giant light bulb lit up. Decades earlier, on an Easter Sunday during a large apartment fire in Pittsburgh, a rescue went badly, and a man fell about thirty feet to his death right in front of me. I'll spare further details, but it was a terrible, unforgettable day. Except I had forgotten . . . sort of. Although the 9/11 pictures instantly provoked a stress reaction, I was blind to the connection. Dave, one of the few people I had ever told about the awful accident, could easily see it. That's an example of the power of social support. His insight started me down a long path of healing.

Today, when I'm triggered, I acknowledge it to myself, take a deep breath, and if it is intense, take it as a signal that I have something to process, which will make me stronger. I still become frustrated at how much work is sometimes required. Talking, writing, and therapy over several years, including an intense conversation with the victim's son, who I hadn't realized was rescued shortly before I arrived, eventually brought me to a point where I can talk about the Easter fire without tears.

MYTH: STRESS REDUCTION

The myth of toxic stress has led to a misguided focus on stress reduction. Parenting is stressful, for example, but how would you go about reducing it? Put some of your children up for adoption? When you see stress as toxic, your goal becomes to get rid of it rather than to embrace it as an essential part of staying strong and healthy. Attempting to avoid stress that way is like avoiding exercise because you are afraid of injury. Without the regular stress of exercise, your muscles atrophy and your bones become brittle. If you don't challenge your brain regularly, your ability to think clearly, learn, and remember suffers. Building strength to manage emotions requires periodic stressful, even painful, transparency and vulnerability.

I have come to believe that teaching people to reduce stress contributes to the rising suicide rate. If people see stress as something to be eliminated, they may see suicide as the ultimate stress reduction.

Three kinds of stress reduction make sense. Using the metaphor of weightlifting, they are:

- Avoiding lifting unsafely or with too much weight (physical—you'll injure your body).
- Avoiding lifting others' weights for them while imagining you are helping (social—you are failing to respect their abilities).
- Avoiding lifting weights so often that you leave no time for renewal (spiritual—your priorities need adjustment).

Creative, adaptive, and flexible responses to stress are literally built into the DNA of living things. When conditions change (as they constantly do), living things discover new ways to cope with the resulting stress.

My childhood neighbor and schoolmate, Frances Arnold, won a Nobel Prize in 2018 (and many other science and engineering honors) for her role in the invention of "directed evolution." She and her colleagues figured out how to stress organisms ("appropriate evolutionary pressure," in her words) to get them to produce desired kinds of enzymes and other proteins so complex that they would be quite difficult to formulate using traditional chemical engineering. The results are microorganisms that can perform chemistry that nature would never have invented, such as turning sugars into fuel and producing new immunotherapies for cancer patients. Directed evolution, with its clever use of stress, has created processes that are far less expensive and more environmentally friendly than their industrial predecessors.

Although stress is essential to health and growth, stress injuries—*traumas*—certainly are real. Our sensitivity to sources of stress—"reactivity," psychologists call it—varies along with our physical, emotional, and spiritual breaking points. Trauma may result from terrible events or chronic danger, neglect, or betrayal. Childhood traumas can be the hardest to heal and are associated with a wide range of physical and mental health issues throughout life, contributing to leading causes of death.[28] Researchers increasingly suspect that too *little* stress during childhood leads to difficulties in adulthood—overprotection, particularly from mothers, has been shown to increase reactivity.[29] Nevertheless, injuries caused by excessive stress can eventually make you stronger, if only because you can end up with greater confidence in your ability to overcome and recover. The phrase "talent needs trauma" in high-performance sports is controversial, but research suggests that those who haven't experienced trauma don't cope with failure as well.[30] Processing past difficulties can make you wiser and more optimistic.[31]

Walking into a support group or a therapist's office no more indicates weakness than walking into a gym or physical therapy. It shows a desire for health and strength. At the end of this book, you'll find some information about recovery from trauma. Physical therapy after injury resembles but isn't the same as exercise. Similarly, psychological and spiritual healing aren't the same as building and maintaining your muscles. Wise people, trained and experienced in mental health and spirituality, can help you choose appropriate "exercises" and a pace that avoids further injury while encouraging healing. But always remember that *you* are the expert on your own life.

Avoiding trauma is wise, but your goal should not be to reduce stress. Seek to gain flexibility so that your stress reactions respond quickly when you need them and quiet quickly when you don't. Teach your stress reactions to fall asleep rapidly by regularly waking up your renewal reactions.

MYTH: RENEWAL FROM STRESS IS SELF-INDULGENCE

Our culture undervalues or ignores the need for renewal, partly because it is our nature to focus on and react to negatives more than positives. Even those of us who commit to mental, emotional, and spiritual "exercise" too often fail to also schedule and commit to the kinds of rest and nourishment that would transform stresses into strengths. But you can't run the race at your best if you don't get rest and nourishment.

The renewal aspects of turning stress into strength are not self-indulgent, although it may look that way as you develop a stronger sense of your own priorities, identity, and boundaries. Conflict with people who expect you to please them is almost inevitable.

It is not pampering yourself or comparing your needs to others. It is about getting what you *need*, not what you want. Renewal—turning stress into strength—is selflessly selfish.

MYTH: STRESS IS A GOOD MOTIVATOR

Although low stress can help you learn simple tasks faster, strong feelings of fear, guilt, or shame will backfire. Even when they seem to be working, it doesn't last. Like any other intense stress, they trigger a threat reaction, shouting down the part of your brain that gives you willpower and impulse control. For example, antismoking campaigns that showed horrible images of lung cancer ultimately led smokers to smoke *more,* not less, as they sought relief from the anxiety that the images inspired. These are only useful motivators if you are trying to provoke people to fight or run away.

MYTH: IT'S ALL ABOUT WILLPOWER OR "MENTAL TOUGHNESS"

Willpower, motivation, impulse control, and self-discipline arise in your brain's prefrontal cortex (PFC), the center of self-discipline, impulse control, willpower, and motivation. Think of it as your internal chief executive officer, a voice of reason that competes with your stress autopilot's emotional, instinct-, and experience-driven urges. Under stress, your autopilot becomes louder, drowning out your PFC. A stuck stress reaction slowly breaks down the connections to your PFC, which can shrink, becoming even more muffled. Meanwhile, your stress autopilot grows bigger and louder, with more neural connections. Its demands—fight, flight, defend, distance, selfish, survivalist—drown out the very traits of willpower and motivation that you need in order to be more resilient.

The balance between your PFC and stress autopilot also depends on genes and life circumstances. Some people are born with more resources and better connections—in their brains, families, or communities. Equal opportunity is an excellent goal, but it remains an ideal more than a reality.

You can grow your PFC and shrink your stress autopilot, making it less sensitive and sticky. Willpower, self-discipline, impulse control, and so forth cannot be the starting point because they are unavailable when you aren't resilient. As you'll read later, the way to form new habits or to end bad ones is by starting small and allowing yourself unlimited permission to fail and start over.

MYTH: RESILIENCE IS SELF-RELIANCE

Becoming more resilient doesn't mean that you, all by yourself, will be ready for whatever life throws your way. Nobody is. Even those who have become self-reliant didn't get that way on their own. Our connections matter, tremendously—in many, many ways, no one is an island, as John Donne famously observed.

Suppose that you have the time and money to prepare for every imaginable difficulty. The unexpected will still happen. To grow more resilient you need to *network,* building and nurturing your connections with things, people, and wisdom. You will become more self-reliant, but you will also become more interdependent.

Although self-reliance frees you from being forced to conform to society's demands, it is a small step away from arrogance and selfishness. Interdependence's gift is to know that you *belong*—to nature, people, and to God or another way you might choose to trust in a higher power. Belonging can also become unhealthy when it becomes codependence that robs others of their self-reliance.

Resilient people are constantly learning and nurturing dependable relationships, while tolerating life's inevitable uncertainty and unpredictability. Your stress autopilot wants to feel that *somebody* dependable is worrying about your safety and needs, but it doesn't always have to be you. You can't do it all.

MYTH: FIGHT STRESS BY GETTING AWAY FROM IT

This is two myths in one. Fighting and fleeing are not renewal, but we sometimes imagine they are.

When you stuff down your stress reactions, you are fighting. You are fighting yourself.

Don't think of stress as something to battle, combat, or any other metaphor for fighting. "What we resist, persists," psychoanalyst Carl Jung observed (and there's plenty of evidence to back him up). Stuffing down your stress is understandable (and sometimes necessary for a time), but exhausting, even though you may be so accustomed to it that you have stopped noticing how tired you are. Choose to begin to learn to welcome and embrace stress, while combining it with renewal, as you'll see in these pages.

When you "check out," you are fleeing.

Rest is critical to renewal, but when distractions and entertainment are ways to avoid or escape necessary stress (like going to the gym), you're still in the flight part of fight or flight. Plopping into the recliner to watch television or play a computer game can easily become a way to avoid being present to yourself and others. Working too much, addictions, and affairs can result in never coming home at all. You won't make progress if avoiding pain is more important to you than growing and staying strong.

Renewal is much more than getting away from the sources of stress. Nourishment also matters. Without social and spiritual rest and nutrition, stress cannot become strength. During true rest and renewal, your body releases hormones and other biological signals that heal stress-caused damage to your heart and other organs.

MYTH: SUCK IT UP AND MOVE ON

Resilience is not about trying harder, even though there are times when "suck it up and move on" is exactly the right thing to do. If you are training for a marathon and feel like quitting after a few miles—suck it up and keep going! Getting out of your comfort zone is essential to building strength. Another saying applies when you are struggling with difficult reactions: "The only way to get rid of bad feelings is to have them." Deciding "I don't want to feel this" dooms you to carry that feeling forever until you change your mind or external events force you to.

realistic optimism

Strong and resilient people are "realistic optimists." Inspirational experts in psychology, coaching, spirituality, and other fields say it various ways, but the idea is the same: those who weather the storms remain hopeful even as they face up to whatever life throws at them, without giving in to despair or denial.

Hope? Optimism? Sounds like someone isn't paying attention. Headlines and social media are filled with violence, war, crime, terrorism, poverty, disease, hate crimes, nasty politics, rudeness, natural disasters. Life across the globe seems to get worse with each passing year.

But if you look at the bigger picture, you'll see that that's wrong.

Even with the world-changing troubles of the COVID-19 pandemic, we are far better off in many ways than our parents, and so is most of the rest of the world. Since 1955, incomes, corrected for inflation, have tripled. Food is much less expensive, more varied, and the possibility of having strangers cook our meals has become affordable to far more people. Today, far fewer of us die in wars, accidents, or from illnesses than ever in history. Poverty has been cut in half since the 1950s. Just 120 years ago, life expectancy was thirty to forty; now it is more than eighty. Crime, violence, and deaths from war have been dropping steadily for decades.

We live far better than *royalty* of a few hundred years ago, given how little we need to work for essentials (food, fuel, clothing, and shelter) and given the choices we have about diet, entertainment, information, transportation, work, and much more.

If life is so much better today, why doesn't it *feel* that way? Why is it such a struggle to be happy and optimistic?

> A pessimist is one who makes difficulties of his opportunities and an optimist is one who makes opportunities of his difficulties.
>
> **—HARRY S. TRUMAN**

Thinking optimistically isn't the same as *feeling* optimistic. Progress and success often fail to make us feel good because our brains react more strongly to bad news than to neutral or positive information. This is the negative bias I mentioned earlier. We are wired to feel our struggles more than our satisfaction. Our brains think it is reasonable to dwell on one negative comment or mistake even when the rest of our day is filled with success. For example, losing often is more upsetting than the happiness we get from winning the equivalent.[1]

Our negative bias interferes with our natural renewal systems. We easily become the opposite of realistic optimists, ignoring our successes and focusing on what is or could go wrong, being mired in excess fear, regrets, resentment, and anxieties. Bad is stronger than good; negative voices are louder, including those in our own heads. But that doesn't mean they must be obeyed. We instinctively see critical people as smarter than positive people, but the squeaky wheel doesn't *always* have to get the grease.

> Your brain is like Velcro for negative experiences and Teflon for positive ones.
>
> **—RICK HANSON**

We reinforce one another's negative biases, being quicker to believe bad news (true or not), better at remembering it, and more eager, clever, and creative about sharing it. When we have something negative to say, we use more words, tell more people, and repeat ourselves more often than when we praise or compliment. If a lot of people have a lot to say about a topic, they are likely to be unhappy, angry, fearful, frustrated, discouraged, or otherwise negative.

At one of the social media intelligence companies I cofounded, we discovered that by counting words and their variety (trivial to compute), we could tell with surprising accuracy if a movie review was positive or negative—people have more to say, with richer vocabulary, when they are negative. We also saw that when more people began to talk about a company, a stock price change often followed, more often down than up. I sometimes regret that I didn't invest based on this observation before it became widely known.

Negative bias helps us survive in a dangerous world, but it is an obstacle to showing up, being present, and enjoying life. To be more resilient, we need to be able to ignore or turn it off when it isn't helpful. But that doesn't come naturally. When one bad thing happens, we illogically feel as though more bad things are likely to happen. We lose our optimism and become more cautious, suspicious, and distrusting. Those are appropriate some of the time, but they wear us down if we get stuck there.

Here is the most important negative bias effect to keep in mind: *most bad things feel worse than they really are.* Negatives get exaggerated. Even the fatigue you feel when you work hard is an exaggeration. You *feel* like you are spent long before you reach your actual limits, because the feeling of fatigue isn't from your muscles; it's a protective emotion from your brain.[2] Mental fatigue is more obviously an emotion because when one kind of task wears you out mentally, you usually will still have plenty of energy for a *different* mental task—playing a challenging game as a break from work, for example.

You are wise to be skeptical of those who stand to profit from tickling your negative bias. No matter what the topic, it is safe to assume that news media, politicians, salespeople, and marketers often exaggerate risk. This doesn't even have to be intentional—those who fail to take advantage of our negative bias are not as successful as those who do; competition tends to weed them out.

Realistic optimism is not just a hope or expectation that things will turn out well; it is fuel for action, a *deep, experience-driven feeling* that things can work for good, that real change for the better is possible, inside and outside of yourself. It is belief, which may or may not be religious, in reconnection, re-creation, and redemption.

stress activators

Your brain's stress autopilot constantly monitors your environment for patterns that signal the possibility of an opportunity, challenge, or threat to *comfort, companionship,* or *meaning.* It doesn't react just to those; it is also sensitive to *affiliation,* on the lookout for the same in the people and things you care about. The more you care, the more it will react. For example, parents are deeply wired to care about their children, so they may even react more strongly to possibilities or harm to a child than to themselves.

The first step toward making your stress reactions more flexible, rather than sticky, is to *notice* what is happening. In this section, my goal is to help you become better at noticing what activates your stress reactions. As you become more aware of stressors and the state of your body and mind, you gain greater power to acknowledge and let go of the reactions when they are not serving you well.

Unless you are unusual, your brain is more sensitive to threats than to opportunities. Even a hint of a significant threat, especially if it touches an unhealed physical or emotional injury, will likely activate your stress autopilot. Its sensitivity increases and you become more reactive if you don't experience renewal after stress. Genetics has built into us some of these autopilot-activating patterns; others we acquire from our experiences.

- Comfort—*Material* needs: health and fitness, food, water, shelter, money, tools, and "muscle memory" skills. Stress activation in this area urges you to protect and care for yourself and others physically—giving you energy to work, to avoid or deal with physical danger, eat when you are hungry, drink when you are thirsty, rest when you are tired, and so forth. If you lack important skills, your stress autopilot will react to what's missing: the feeling of control that comes from mastery.

- Companionship—*Social* needs: friends, mentors, pets, leaders, status, reputation, as well as language and information that others provide. Stress activation in this area makes you feel suspicious of strangers, critical, ignored, embarrassed, excluded, unloved, abandoned, disrespected, distrusted, or lonely. Social stress is also triggered by grief, isolation, and worrying about what others think of you.

- Meaning—*Spiritual* needs: faith, values, wisdom, morals, ethics—thoughts and feelings that are rooted less in logic and more in love, compassion, and right or wrong. This helps you to choose goals, priorities, and values, to decide what you say yes or no to. Stress activation in this area makes your life seem empty, lacking meaning or purpose. Spiritual stress can be especially difficult when something that is "not supposed to happen" happens anyway, or something that is "supposed to happen" doesn't. When you violate a "supposed to," feeling guilt or shame is normal. When others do so, you may feel manipulated, betrayed, passionless, trapped, or even bored.

Your stress autopilot is emotional and automatic, not logical or deliberate. You were born knowing some life-enhancing and lifesaving patterns (for example, staying away from the edge of a cliff); you have absorbed others from your experiences. Even when there isn't any actual risk, your autopilot may react to situations that resemble past stressful ones. If you were frequently criticized as a child and had to earn your parents' affections, for example, your autopilot might regard getting any kind of feedback as a pattern calling for an automatic, defensive stress reaction. On the other hand, you may also instinctively trust and be drawn to people who resemble those who loved and cared for you (even when the resemblance is something you dislike).

The power of patterns to activate emotions is why fiction— books, movies, theater, simulations, and so forth—can make you happy, amused, sad, angry, frightened, or anxious, even though they are not literally true.

Stress activators can sneak up on you because your autopilot is far better at controlling than communicating. Its "thought process" is available to us only through dreams, instinct, intuition, and other nonverbal information.

Sensory reminders also can activate your stress reactions—if you are a war veteran who smelled burning oil wells during combat, you might grow tense at the odor of an asphalt plant. It's not logical, just a familiar pattern. You may not even realize what provoked the reaction. Smells are especially powerful, but sights, sounds, stories, and even the calendar can activate a stress reaction.

Identification is a stress activator that can be difficult to recognize—you are wired to react to opportunities, challenges, or threats to people who resemble you or those you care about. For example, if you have a ten-year-old child, you almost certainly will feel a stronger stress reaction to seeing or hearing about injury or threat to a ten-year-old than somebody who doesn't have a child that age. The greater the similarities, the stronger your reaction is likely to be. This can sneak up on you, as when your autopilot identifies with someone who resembles you in a way you don't want to admit about yourself.

Unpredictability is a stress activator because it conflicts with your brain's emotional desire for control. Your autopilot may strongly urge you to avoid the possibility of a negative surprise. You may tolerate or even seek out familiar, yet bad, experiences, re-creating unhealthy relationships and repeating mistakes rather than take a chance on the new and unknown. As the following story shows, even when an unpredictable event is in your favor, you can feel distress.

My friend felt responsible for a zip-line accident. He was clipping people onto the line, but his youth organization hadn't fully trained him. He used the wrong harness loop on a big adult and it broke. The man fell twenty-five feet and barely survived.

The victim sued. Lawyers assured my friend that, as a volunteer for a nonprofit, there was no chance he would be held personally responsible. The parties settled out of court and that was the end of it. Yet, a couple of years later, he told me that the most difficult part for him was that there were no real consequences, no penalty (even though being sued and deposed had been stressful).

My friend's brain, longing for predictability, was saying, "If you hurt someone, punishment should follow." Anything else is unpredictable and therefore deserves a stress reaction.

Your autopilot influences your thinking far more than your thoughts can influence your autopilot. This book is not about controlling or ignoring your stress autopilot. Trying to control it is exhausting. Trying to ignore it is paralyzing. *Own it,* because it is not just a fearful, primitive, wild animal trapped in your modern mind, messing up your plans and priorities. Your stress reactions drive excitement, passion, achievement, romance, strength, growth, and much more, because, again, fear is not the only thing that makes our hearts race!

"your brain will do that"

My crisis intervention instructors included Dr. George S. Everly Jr., of Johns Hopkins University, one of the founders of the International Critical Incident Stress Foundation. Everly's oft-repeated phrase, "Your brain will do that," lodged deep in my mind. I have found myself repeating it to people in crisis when they wonder if they are going crazy.

My hope for you, as you read this chapter, is that you'll come to appreciate that, as annoying, frustrating, and even angering as our stress reactions can be sometimes, they are what human brains do—and there's always a good reason for them.

> Courage is resistance to fear, mastery of fear—not absence of fear.
>
> —MARK TWAIN

During challenge and threat reactions, stress hormones flow, your heart beats faster, digestion slows down, your sense of time alters, memory sharpens, and other physical and mental changes prepare you for action. Your thoughts, emotions, body, and behavior change.

THINKING AND MEMORY CHANGE

Stress can temporarily improve your eyesight but also can give you "tunnel vision." Although emotionally you may be reacting to past stress or worrying about the future, your attention shifts toward the source of stress and what *might* result. Stress-driven thinking is rigid, perfectionist, this-or-that, all-or-nothing, and judgmental. Careful analysis and thoughtfulness easily get "drowned out" by stress. Don't believe everything you think, so that you aren't reacting to what *might h*appen instead of what *is* happening.

Stress causes your brain to shift into "possibility thinking," imagining what might happen, rather than just considering what *probably* will. Possibility thinking can be powerful. It keeps people safe in hazardous environments and can drive creativity and innovation. Silicon Valley's venture capital community makes an industry out of considering long-shot possibilities that most investors would consider too risky. But getting stuck in a habit of seizing opportunities has also been the downfall of many entrepreneurs who spread their companies too thin. Businesses that don't focus their limited resources on solving just one important problem often fail.

Combine possibility thinking with a heightened negative bias from repeated exposure to threats, and you can end up struggling to stop your brain from dwelling on what *might* go wrong. Your brain will do that, having learned from experience, but getting stuck in possibility thinking is annoying, distracting, and exhausting. You can end up missing opportunities, weighed down by being prepared for "everything" (but you're not).

Seeing choices other than your automatic habits is difficult under stress. I had an opportunity to "drive" a San Jose Police Department highly realistic police driving simulator. In my final scenario, I chased a bad guy through city streets until he bailed out at a shopping center. There he was, pointing a pistol at me, and began shooting. Bullet holes began appearing in my windshield. I had no idea what to do. The training officer behind me started yelling, "Run him over! Run his ass over right now!" It seemed entirely wrong. It didn't help that a little voice in my head was saying, "I was a paramedic, I don't kill people, I save them." It was paralyzing, but eventually I stomped on the gas and ran him over. Even though it was a simulation, it was unforgettable and unpleasant.

Muscle memory can give you fast reflexes, but it can lead to unavoidable errors when you face a situation similar to but different from your stress autopilot's experience-based programming. For example, point something vaguely gun-shaped at a cop in a dark alley and the officer's trained, automatic reaction may mean that you won't survive because our stress autopilots prompt literally "thought-less" instant reactions. Officers who aren't trained to react instantly might not survive a similar experience with a real gun.

"That's the way we've always done it," which could be a stress autopilot's motto, has been called the most dangerous phrase in organizational management. The same can be true for us individually. Although now you may think like an adult (most of the time, anyway), when your autopilot takes over, it often falls back on patterns your brain absorbed during childhood, which typically don't work well in the adult world. I'll dive deeper into that topic in an upcoming chapter that describes how your greatest gifts are also your biggest obstacles when you overuse them.

Your memory improves under stress. That's why moderate stimulants, such as coffee, help you remember what you study but must be used with caution because they interfere with sleep, which is essential to retaining memories. You almost certainly have strong memories of negative social experiences, such as your most embarrassing moments, or any time you were seriously injured. Your brain will do that—the more stressful the experience, the more your autopilot will demand that you remember and learn or make meaning from it. For example, nearly all of us who were past preschool on November 22, 1963, remember what we were doing when John F. Kennedy was assassinated. The same is true for those who were old enough to be aware of the events of September 11, 2001.

The excitement that accompanies an especially good experience (which can trigger a stress reaction) also improves memory. Although it may seem easier to recall memories of bad events, you are unlikely to forget your first kiss, the birth of a child, or a major achievement. Your brain wants you to learn and be changed by those too.

The more threatened you feel (for yourself or anything you care about), the more your brain will store, analyze, and "replay" details—sights, sounds, smells, and other sensory data. If the threat is intense or long lasting, you will tend to stay on alert, prepared for fight or flight. Sticky stress is wired into us for safety in the present; detailed memories are wired into us for safety in the future. If you spotted a tiger, it may still be there and it may come back later. We are wired to be often wrong about danger rather than to take a chance on letting down our guard. That's possibility thinking.

Recalling unwanted bad memories can feel intrusive and seem useless ("Can't change the past"). If you feel that way, remind yourself that your brain is earning its paycheck, urging you to learn or make meaning from whatever happened. But one of the benefits of exposure to intermittent moderate adversity is that it can make you better at forgetting difficult experiences.[3]

> I remember the old man who said he had had a great many troubles in his life, but the worst of them never happened.
>
> —JAMES A. GARFIELD

Although learning from experiences allows us to predict and prepare, our tendency to ruminate—replaying the past and re-hearsing future risky situations—will backfire if it is self-punishing. Positive self-criticism is helpful; when it triggers guilt or shame, our stress reaction sticks.

Commuting by bicycle in Silicon Valley for a few years was good for my physical health, but it felt risky. It seemed like I was invisible to many drivers. Although no one hit me, I had close calls. I'd find myself replaying them in my head, angry at the careless driver. The irony is that when I was lost in my fear-driven angry thoughts, I was less safe because I was no longer paying attention to traffic! Eventually I'd notice where my brain had gone, which allowed me to let go of the anger and return to the present, alert to new threats, while able to enjoy my ride more.

Unrelieved stress can also lead to dangerous thrill-seeking. The only time I got hurt on a bike was my own fault—I hit a pothole on a trail and flew over the handlebars, dislocating my shoulder. There was, a strong tailwind and my last thought before the accident was, "I wonder how fast I can go."

When feeling stressed leads you to "check out," you're still in fight-or-flight mode, whether it's happening on the bike trail or over dinner with your spouse. Employers have a word for showing up for work but not really being there—instead of "absenteeism," they call it "presenteeism."

EMOTION CHANGES

When stress hormones flood your body, it is normal to feel excited, anxious, or scared, depending on how much of a challenge or threat your autopilot perceives the activating event to be. Those feelings can help you to focus better, react faster, and even enjoy the ecstasy of engagement. Long-term stress activation can leave you defensive, moody, angry, depressed, grouchy, uninspired, and easily distracted, acting more from negative feelings than from rational thoughts. Major threats can make you feel overwhelmed, out of control, or helpless. To feel like you have some control, you might blame others or yourself, feeling guilty or ashamed about an event you could not control, such as feeling like the 9/11 attacks were your fault because you didn't pray hard enough (an actual example I encountered).

Conspiracy theories and rumors make more sense when you look at them through the lens of control. For example, if the COVID-19 virus came from a random mutation, we have no control over that. But if we believe it was created intentionally in a laboratory, that tells our stress autopilot that it is possible to stop future pandemics, which in turn creates a sense of control and predictability. This doesn't mean all conspiracy theories are false, but it is good reason to remain skeptical.

As stress makes us more selfish and survivalist, our social behavior can change dramatically. We become more tribal, suspicious, and distrustful of anybody we think of as "them" and not "us," which could be based in politics, race, family, or any other grouping. Either-this-or-that, binary thinking also contributes to tribalism, leaving little room for anyone to be in between: "You are either for us or against us." Under extreme threat, we may only look out for ourselves.

PHYSIOLOGY CHANGES

During a stress reaction, your metabolism revs up. This is like shifting your car into low gear and stomping on the gas pedal—it gives you more power. But you don't want to get stuck in low gear because it uses a lot more fuel and wears you down. Stress can mask pain, but when your stress response sticks, it can cause excess anxiety, aches and pains, digestive problems, chest pain, rapid heart rate, illness, and a loss of sex drive, sometimes even weeks or months later. (But remember that, unlike your car, your body can repair itself when you activate renewal!)

The stickiness of your stress response means that the associated hormones—adrenaline and cortisol, in particular—can remain elevated long after the source of the stress is gone. Continuously high cortisol levels are bad for your physical health and break down a part of your brain closely involved with learning and memory,[4] including social memory, such as associating faces with names.[5] Sustained elevated stress hormones lead to cardiovascular disease, type 2 diabetes, and a number of other illnesses. The negative effects can compound one another. For example, high cortisol levels will make you crave carbohydrates. A high-carbohydrate diet will cause you to gain weight, which can cause or aggravate sleep apnea, further raising your cortisol levels. It can be a vicious circle, fouling up your body's signals for hunger and fullness, leading to loss of appetite or overeating and weight gain.

BEHAVIOR CHANGES

Chronic or intense stress activation can lead you to sleep too much or too little, withdraw from social events, procrastinate, abuse substances, struggle to think clearly, or find yourself with nervous habits. In an unconscious effort to avoid feeling helpless, you may become more of a perfectionist, or you may become more rigid, profoundly uncomfortable with uncertainty, cynical, suspicious, blaming, and distrusting of anyone or anything that is new, unfamiliar, or different. When your stress autopilot drowns out your brain's centers of motivation and willpower, you are more impulsive and less self-disciplined. Shopping while your stress autopilot is activated (including when hungry, of course) can be expensive!

Stress reactions can be cumulative. It's as if you carry a stress "backpack" and each event adds another rock to the pack. The weight increases slowly, so you may not even notice it until one day you realize that you are always tired. Carrying a heavy pack can make you strong, but that strength only develops if you regularly unload, rest, and get nourishment. You must experience renewal to unload the backpack and gain benefit from stress.

The nature and intensity of these stress autopilot-prompted changes depend on your autopilot's sense of your ability to maintain control. You might react to an event as a challenge or a threat.

GUT-LEVEL CONFIDENCE DRIVES CHALLENGE REACTIONS

When stress hits and you are confident—not just in your head, but in your gut—that you can cope with change or adversity, you are stressed but *excited*. A challenge reaction gives you courage and conviction. Embrace it. Research shows that people perform better when they feel some stress, rather than being totally relaxed—especially if they choose to see their stress reactions as helpful.[6] "Coping" can mean solving a problem, dealing with the emotions it triggers, or both.

FEAR DRIVES THREAT REACTIONS

When you face a threat and feel less confident, or when life seems out of control and you feel helpless or alone, you have a "threat" reaction. You may become pale and scared as blood shifts inward (this will help stop bleeding if you are injured). Your blood pressure spikes, sending fuel to your brain and other vital organs. The stress autopilot takes charge, and you struggle to think clearly or creatively because the emotion-driven urge to fight or flee is overpowering the logical part of your brain. During an extreme threat reaction, you may even freeze, paralyzed and unable to respond at all.

When a situation begins to feel overwhelming, *fearing* stress only makes things worse. Instead, embrace it. Recall that your automatic reactions help you focus and react quickly. Tell yourself, "This is my brain and body rising to the occasion, helping me." Although you can't simply decide to make something a challenge instead of a threat, you can help your brain's rational voice compete with your stress autopilot's worried clamor.

renewal activators

Our renewal reactions activate when we connect and commit to things (physical), people (social), and values (spiritual), ideally as a generous giver and grateful receiver of comfort, companionship, and meaning. These relationships shape us; the stronger they are, the more energy we give one another.

If you have experienced intense or long-lasting stress without adequate renewal, your brain and body will have changed, making activation of your renewal reactions more difficult. Be patient and know that progress never follows a straight line. It is more like spaghetti. Your hormone levels need time to shift. The part of your brain that reacts to stress—your autopilot—needs time to shrink and disconnect, while your brain's center of learning, decision-making, self-discipline, and motivation (your PFC) needs time to grow and reconnect. There are few quick fixes. Expect setbacks; know that they are normal and inevitable. Give yourself unlimited permission to fail and start over.

Physical renewal activators ("rest and digest") include safety, relaxation, rest, comfort food, sleep, nutrition, shelter, and the security that comes from having things you need. You can trigger physical renewal with deep breathing, connection with nature (gardening, hiking, trash pickup), touch, dance, sports, music, drumming, and mind-body practices such as yoga, Pilates, tai chi, or practicing "muscle memory" tasks and tools.

Social renewal activators ("tend and befriend") have to do with companionship and social bonding—people and animals (especially dogs and horses) whose presence is reassuring, those whom you can "get real" with, letting down your guard so that you are free to be yourself and talk about what really matters (such as teachers, coaches, and mentors). Eye contact, touch, empathy, playfulness, acknowledgment, sharing meals, and team and group activities from sports to singing can activate renewal. Social renewal helps you to process thoughts and emotions, to share information and knowledge.

Spiritual renewal activators ("pause and plan") include compassion for yourself and others, freedom to fail without judgment, tapping into your sense of awe and wonder, choosing priorities, and forgiveness. Spiritual renewal helps you know and maintain your priorities and moral compass.

Rituals, religious and secular, often combine physical, social, and spiritual renewal activators. Rituals can signal an important connection or rite of passage, such as marriage, birth, election or appointment, or joining a team. They also mark disconnection— in grief, we naturally feel an urge to gather with our family and "tribe" (the renewal hormone oxytocin prompts us), creating symbols and actions that express and acknowledge our shared loss. We celebrate birthdays to remind one another of our connections and observe holidays to stay connected with nature's rhythms. On the surface, many modern rituals seem like little more than entertainment, although some take them quite seriously—Monday Night Football, events such as "Burning Man," and so forth.

Renewal is less sensitive and sticky than stress, so you have to make more of an effort to activate it. Just getting away from the sources of stress doesn't activate renewal, nor do casual encounters with nature, people, and values. Renewal is prompted by *connections with commitment* because your autopilot needs to sense *dependability* in yourself and others. For example, physical activators include *deep* sleep and *deep* breathing; social activators need *strong and faithful* relationships; spiritual activators require *engagement* with wisdom and values. Shallow doesn't do it. You can't fool your autopilot into "knowing" something you have not experienced.

renewal effects on the brain and body

Endless books and advice are available to describe our physical and mental stress reactions. Our renewal reactions (rest and digest, tend and befriend, pause and plan) get much less attention. They quiet the stress reactions while promoting healing and growth.

Renewal has the same dimensions as stress: rest and digest is a *comfort* renewal activator, tend and befriend is a *companionship* activator, and pause and plan is a *meaning* activator.

Just as your body automatically produces stress hormones, you have renewal hormones—oxytocin, vasopressin, androgens, growth hormone, DHEA, and others. They trigger growth and repair of the damage done during stressful periods. Physical stress causes damage; renewal hormones trigger healing and growth. During downtime, you digest food, heal and grow muscles, strengthen bones, and go through myriad other repair and growth processes. But the healing and growth prompted by renewal activation are not just physical.

Emotional and mental stress can break down social bonds; renewal hormones drive us to rebuild and strengthen them.[7] Your thoughts and emotions calm down and rebuild, so that you can process memories, organize information, let go of worries, connect with companions, internalize wisdom, and much more. For example, the renewal hormone oxytocin influences our instinct to gather with friends and family during periods of joy or grief; higher levels make us more willing to share our emotions and recognize what others are feeling, strengthening our social bonds.[8] When we activate renewal, we make more eye contact, become better at distinguishing friend or foe, and more easily identify emotions from facial expressions—all of which correlate to higher oxytocin levels.[9] Conversely, the more our stress autopilot is activated, the less likely we are to see *anyone* as a trustworthy friend.

It is worth noting that stress and renewal hormones are not identical in males and females (not just in humans but in mammals in general). Females produce more oxytocin, and males produce more androgens, such as testosterone. Higher oxytocin levels make you more social and caring, seeking the company and support of your family, friends, and "tribe," so it isn't surprising that women have a stronger tend-and-befriend renewal reaction. Men tend to retreat to their "caves," with a greater need for solitude. These are generalizations; individuals vary greatly. Men also tend and befriend, women also withdraw. Introverts draw more energy from solitude, extroverts draw more from social support.

Oxytocin is released during stress, but unlike the other stress hormones, its continued release helps activate renewal and protect you from the negative effects of stress.[10] Although this is an oversimplification, chronically elevated stress hormones are inflammatory and damage your cardiovascular system; renewal hormones are generally anti-inflammatory and protect and repair your body, including the heart muscle.[11] Chronic inflammation is linked to many common physical and mental ailments.

Renewal happens when you can let down your guard and relax. You worry less about possibilities and become more thoughtful, contemplative, compassionate, kind, patient, flexible, and generous. You are less likely to react automatically and more free to take a moment, or even count to ten, before responding to a frustration or irritant. In other words, renewal from stress gives you more choices, to be more flexible, creative, and innovative in response to what life deals you. When you are struggling with a problem, letting go of it and activating renewal can trigger a breakthrough. Often, solving a problem or figuring out how to seize an opportunity happens unconsciously—how many times has "sleeping on it" led to a flash of insight?

Creative people have wide-ranging interests and give their attention to things that on the surface would seem to have nothing to do with their focus. Seeing from others' points of view can be a powerful agent of change. During renewal, our brains have an uncanny ability to assemble existing ideas into new inventions.

the "wolves" in your nervous system

An old man is teaching his grandson about life. "A fight is going on inside me," he says to the boy.

"It is a terrible fight and it is between two wolves. One is bad—he is anger, envy, sorrow, regret, greed, arrogance, self-pity, guilt, resentment, inferiority, lies, false pride, superiority, and ego. The other is good—he is joy, peace, love, hope, serenity, humility, kindness, benevolence, empathy, generosity, truth, compassion, and faith. The same fight is going on inside you—and inside every other person too."

The grandson thinks about it for a minute and then asks his grandfather, "Which wolf will win?"

The old man replies, "The one you feed."

The fable, often attributed to the Cherokee, is a remarkably accurate description of the shouting match that happens within each of us during stress reactions. The "bad" wolf is your *sympathetic nervous system,* the autopilot that triggers your fight-or-flight response. This wolf is an ally when you need to rise to a challenge or cope with a threat. The bad wolf is suspicious, aggressive, easily angered, and focuses on immediate risks, without regard for long-term consequences. You don't have to feed your bad wolf—he takes what he wants! He is bad for you only when he stays in charge when no longer needed.

Get to know your bad wolf. He protects you from more than just *external* threats; he also protects you from pain you carry inside. When he sniffs a situation that signals challenge, danger, or opportunity, he wakes up to give you stamina, focus, and other coping abilities—fight or flight, defend or distance, selfish or survivalist. All of those reactions are gifts to help you get by in a world of opportunities and risks. As you'll read later, they become liabilities only when you overuse them.

The "good" wolf is your parasympathetic nervous system, which tells your body it is time to renew itself, your rest-and-digest, tend-and-befriend, and pause-and-plan responses. It includes the vagus nerve, the body's biggest, sometimes called the brain-body intercom. The more active your vagus nerve is, the more resilient you are. Renewal strengthens your neural and hormonal "relax, it's safe" messages, your vagus nerve's ability to send them, and your brain and body's ability to receive them.

> The person we long to be—and already are, deep down—is usually covered over with stresses, distractions, fears and regrets.
>
> **—RICK HANSON**

Our biggest mistake is thinking we can starve the bad wolf. Television, video games, social media, shopping, alcohol, drugs, affairs, jobs—when you use these to escape, it backfires. You become more isolated, exhausted, detached, and apathetic. Although downtime is essential to renewal, escapism feeds your bad wolf and starves your good wolf.

Confronting escapist behavior, your own or another's, you may declare, "Just start making better choices." That won't work because blame and shame feed your bad wolf, which is making the best choices it can. Better choices become possible only when you regularly feed your good wolf, allowing your body, mind, and spirit to renew and grow.

no comparison stress shopping allowed

Although I introduced this book by comparing life today to earlier times, the point was that comparisons are not helpful. Avoid them. Life is messy. Comparisons to others are misleading. People share their triumphs, successes, resentments, and outrage far more than their failures and shortcomings. This has always been true. But with social media, people are broadcasting their accomplishments, outrages, and lopsided projections faster and much more widely. Comparing yourself to the boasts of social media friends or, worse, to celebrities will do little more than build up your resentments and tear down your self-esteem.

The trials and failures of celebrities and strangers remain invisible until their bankruptcy, divorce, addiction, or other struggle becomes too big to hide. As you wrestle with your life's challenges, *don't compare yourself to anyone else.* You have no idea what troubles go with others' successes—and someone else will always be wealthier, more powerful, better looking, or otherwise ahead of you.

As Janet Childs puts it, "No comparison stress shopping!"

To paraphrase a teenage friend who lived with an incurable illness, adversity isn't a bump in the road, it *is* the road. We don't overcome obstacles so that we can get back to living our lives; obstacles are part of life.

One day in the 1990s, I stepped onto an elevator at the Las Vegas Hilton just after arriving for COMDEX, the world's biggest computer industry conference. There was Bill Gates—same age as me, working in the same industry, infinitely more financially successful, with more money than anybody else. We were acquainted because I was helping Microsoft with product strategy. I'm not great at small talk, and my frequent opening line when I saw people I know in Vegas was, "So, do you gamble when you come here?" I was about to ask Bill that question when I realized how completely different gambling must be when you don't have to worry about your personal finances. I stopped myself and just said, "Hi, Bill." I have held on to that moment as a lesson that comparing myself to other people is a path to unhappiness.

guilt, shame, and the "shoulds"

Make the word *should* a red flag when you are dealing with change, stress, or trauma, especially grief and loss. As you struggle to make a new routine into a habit, or end a bad habit, the feeling "I *should* do X" is natural. But when you notice yourself doing that, acknowledge it and set it aside. Letting go of shoulds has nothing to do with right and wrong. You still should do the right thing. I'm talking about the kind of shoulds that leave you feeling anxious, guilty, or ashamed. In fact, the word *should* is derived from ancient terms for guilt and owing money!

Feeling guilt or shame is natural. There's a name for those who lack the conscience that gives rise to these emotions— psychopaths. Accept what you feel, but don't let it tell you who you really are. Remind yourself that you feel guilt or shame because the true "you" knows something is wrong. But they are not healthy motivators. They might seem to work in the short run, but because they are based in stress and fear, they will *erode* your motivation, enthusiasm, and self-discipline.[12] To grow, you need periodic freedom from them.

Here's a way to gain some insight into whether or not a should—something you feel guilt or shame about—is healthy. Ask yourself, "Is this an ethical or moral issue?"

For example, the decision to go work out at the gym is not ethical or moral. Neither is eating a big bag of potato chips or failing to make an appointment for a medical checkup. Unfortunately, we often treat such behaviors and their consequences as moral failures. Overweight? That condition has far more to do with stressful experiences than morals. Addicted? Ditto. Easily distracted? Same. Psychologists who specialize in stress and trauma have learned that the question "What happened to you?" is far preferable to "What is wrong with you?"

Procrastination is often our favorite way to avoid feeling guilt and shame when we "should on ourselves"—but then we inevitably feel guilt and shame about procrastinating! As Admiral Ackbar exclaimed in *Star Wars: Return of the Jedi*: "It's a trap!"

I used to have a recurring should dream (a mild nightmare, really) about returning an overdue library book. The longer I put off returning the book, the more anxious I'd feel, so I'd distract myself by doing something more pleasant. The book would become even more overdue, and my anxiety, already out of proportion, would become worse. That's the should-ing on yourself trap. It makes things worse, not better.

> The only person you should compete with is the person you were yesterday.
>
> **—PREM JAGYASI**

Stress-driven, this-or-that thinking—seeing everything as either good or bad—easily turns guilt into shame. The unfortunate logic of a stress-activated brain says that doing something bad makes you a bad person. Renewal from stress will help change your thinking from the binary either-or to an inclusive both-and. You'll have a much easier time accepting the truth that you are a good person who did a bad thing (guilt) rather than forming the self-destructive conviction that you are bad person (shame). As you build strength and resilience, binary thinking will give way to healthier dual thinking. For example, changing a diaper shows love, but . . . yuck! When you engage deeply with life, you'll find it inevitably includes some horrible, or at least uncomfortable, privileges.

The phrase *horrible privilege* came from my last day on the devastating 2015 Valley Fire in Lake County. I was providing peer support and crisis intervention as a contractor for Cal Fire's Employee Support Services (ESS) team. On our final day, my partner, Chris Curtis, and I went to the small community of Anderson Springs as it was reopened to residents, many of whom had lost everything. We noticed a family beginning to sift through the rubble where their house had been, so I walked to them to see if I could assist.

As I approached, I saw a young woman kneeling near the remains of the house, sobbing. I came up behind her and gently put a hand on her back without saying anything. After a little while, imagining she was reacting to the reality that her home was gone, I knelt down with her and said something like, "It's really hard to see, isn't it?"

She cried harder, then stood up and managed to say, "Our animals!"

I looked in front of us and saw fences and realized this was where they had kept their pets, which were trapped in the fire. Chris and I love dogs. The nightmare we were seeing hit very close to home.

Over the next hour or so, Chris and I helped that family recover and bury the remains of four dogs. We also managed to dig urns containing their grandparents' ashes out of the rubble of the house. They told us that those were the two tasks they had in mind that day—bury the dogs, find the urns.

The sights and smells were almost overwhelming, but so was their gratitude. They hugged us and insisted we pose for a picture with them. The task was horrible—I kept praying that my brain would not replay the images or odors. Yet it was an honor to help that family. Allowing an experience like this to be both horrible and a privilege, rather than giving into the shoulds (dogs should not suffer, people should not have to lose their dogs, we should not have to see and smell such things, and so on), is how we practice the essential resilience habit of acceptance. There is nothing easy about doing so. To process that experience, I talked with friends and wrote about it. This may seem odd, but the most comforting thing anyone said to me afterward came from Chief Mike Ming, who now is the head of ESS: "Sounds like you did what needed to be done." Exactly.

As you aspire to let go of your shoulds, avoid generalizing (which has the terrible effect of turning guilt into shame) and convert them into something positive. Be specific and include the *why* behind them. In the long run, goals are far more powerful than guilt. For example, instead of "I should get more exercise," try "I will go to the gym today so that I feel more energy and stay healthy." When you notice that a should is sneaking up on you, try substituting the words *choose* or *want*. For example, instead of "I should exercise today," try, "I *choose* (or want) to exercise today."

Ask yourself if you are stuck because you think you *should* make a certain choice, or you want to please somebody other than yourself. Check in with your body. If the choice feels like it is coming from your head, it may still be a should. If it feels right, it's more likely to truly be your choice, your desire.

A simple research project revealed a way to help you say no more easily. A group that was told to say "I can't" gave into temptation 61 percent of the time. But a group that was told to say "I don't" gave in 36 percent of the time.[13] They also found that this kind of "reframing" helps with motivation. Eight out of ten members of a group that was told to say "I *don't* miss workouts" stuck to their goal, compared with only one out of ten of those who said "I *can't* miss my workout." The "can't" group performed *worse* than the control group, which had no temptation-avoidance strategy and in which three out of ten stuck to their goal.

Why is this language change so powerful? Consider what it means to say "I can't." Who is in control? Not you, apparently. It implies that you would say yes if you could, but for some reason you cannot. On the other hand, "I don't" firmly puts you in the driver's seat, choosing and committing to what you will or will not do. As you've learned, feeling helpless or out of control activates your stress autopilot, robbing you of willpower, motivation, and self-discipline. The language you choose can activate or quiet that stress autopilot. Choose language that puts *you* in charge of your life.

If a should is hard to ignore, ask yourself where you learned it and if *you*, the true you, agrees. Is it really a priority? Is it really what *you* want? What are you saying yes to? Where is the pressure coming from? Ask yourself, "Who's talking?" Is it the true you, or the wounded, fearful you? Naming the sources of shoulds can take away their power to limit your choices.

Be gentle with yourself. We tend to be so much harder on ourselves than the people around us. Letting go of the strongest shoulds, the ones you have carried for a long time, is hard. They never silence altogether, but you can build up the power to acknowledge and let them go.[14]

Fear, worry, guilt, anger, and anxiety are temporary, natural, and healthy reactions to stressful events, but they hold you back when they no longer serve a positive purpose. You cannot ignore or think them away. You can "power through" them for a while, but it is exhausting and eventually fails. They are insidious because you can become so accustomed to living with them that you may stop noticing them. Over time, resilience routines, especially compassion for yourself and others, will help take away their power to distract and sabotage you.

> Knowledge is important, but only if we're being kind and gentle with ourselves as we work to discover who we are.
>
> — BRENÉ BROWN, *The Gifts of Imperfection*

Have compassion for yourself; accept your struggles and reactions as natural and necessary, but don't idealize normalcy. Carrying on with "business as usual" will take you nowhere. Resilience routines are going to create a new normal for you. Being kind to yourself is powerful. Unfortunately, many of us scold ourselves like comedian Bob Newhart in a hilarious portrayal of a terrible (but quick!) psychotherapist, who charges $10 to shout at his patients, "Just stop it!"[15]

As I have said to people in crisis many times, "Consider treating yourself as gently as you would a friend struggling with the same thing." What would you say to that friend? Would you tell them they only have themselves to blame? Would you say, "Just get over it"? I hope not—and I urge you to be just as kind to yourself. Compassion isn't coddling.

> When we fail we are merely joining the great parade of humanity that has walked ahead of us and will follow after us.
>
> **—RICHARD ROHR**

Anything that helps you build strength involves stress, including developing a new habit. The biggest enemy of building strength and resilience may be the idea that you *should not* have to feel stress. Accept, don't condemn, your stress reactions, including guilt and shame. Remind yourself that they are helping you rise to the challenge of becoming more resilient! Everyone struggles with stepping out of their comfort zones, so remember: *Just start over. Never interpret a temporary setback as a permanent character flaw.* You have unlimited permission to fail and start over.

> The secret of getting ahead is getting started. The secret of getting started is breaking your complex overwhelming tasks into small manageable tasks, and then starting on the first one.
>
> **—ANONYMOUS**

Sometimes, even starting over is too difficult. Yes, I'm giving you permission to procrastinate. Except that's not true—I'm giving you permission to *be gentle with yourself* when you aren't doing what you imagine you should. Self-judgment—condemning yourself for failure—is normal and natural, but get in the habit of acknowledging and setting it aside so that you can start small and start over.

Willpower does not grow overnight any more than muscles do. Give your self-control muscles some exercise by practicing with minor things that you are confident you can do (or not do). Walk past the bowl of jellybeans. Park a little farther from the door so you get some more steps in. You are rewiring your brain, which takes time, exercise, rest, and nourishment, just like growing muscles.

Guilt and shame can be chains that keep you from coming home. That's because "home" is never a place where everybody is good; it's the place where everybody is broken. Nobody is eager to be a poster child for brokenness, but nothing connects us more deeply than acknowledging that we all belong to that club. Sharing our failures with trusted companions creates compassion, the antidote to guilt and shame.

obstacles to renewal— living disconnected

Don't beat yourself up for feeling stressed, anxious, and not resilient enough—you are far from alone. Renewal does not come easily today. Although we are living in the most technologically connected culture that has ever existed, isolation, inactivity, and meaninglessness are on the rise. The modern world is so disconnected from sources of renewal that many people don't even realize what is missing. They just know they are anxious and, saddest of all, lonely—some profoundly so.

An astonishing 40 percent of American adults report feeling lonely. Millions of people, especially men, have *zero* close friends. Loneliness rates have doubled since the 1980s. Ask a therapist what problems they encounter each day and you will hear that loneliness and its cousin, anxiety, top the list, by far.

Loneliness is lethal. Researchers have found that it dramatically raises heart disease and stroke rates, increasing your risk of early death more than smoking or high blood pressure, taking an average of ten years off your life.[1] It is also expensive—the U.S. government spends an estimated $6.7 billion annually to address social isolation in older adults. Vivek Murthy, the former U.S. surgeon general, says that the most concerning health issue in the United States is not cancer, heart disease, or obesity. It is isolation.

Loneliness does not just mean being alone. You can be surrounded by people, interacting with them regularly, yet not truly be connected to them.

"Loneliness does not come from having no people about one but from being unable to communicate the things that seem important to oneself, or from holding certain views which others find inadmissible," psychoanalyst Carl Jung observed.

Our disconnection is not just social. We are also disengaged from helpful physical stress and renewal. Nearly a third of the world's population is physically inactive.[2] Compared with our predecessors, we work out less, eat worse, get less sleep, gain more debt, pay to store more stuff, and generate more trash. Also disengaged spiritually, we are more cynical and less inspired and motivated. We skip reassuring rituals and "go it alone" rather than being mentored or mentoring, while allowing money and power to trump higher values and meaning.

Loneliness, as serious as it is, may not be as big a problem as another that science has discovered is a significant contributor to isolation, infection, pain, accidents, obesity, cancer, diabetes, Alzheimer's, heart disease, stroke, depression, anxiety, and suicide. What is this terrible thing with a strong relationship to illness, injury, and all major causes of death? It is a lack of the most profound type of *rest* in life's melody: sleep. Want to lose weight? First make sure you are getting enough sleep. Want to reduce cancer's aggressiveness and the odds of getting it in the first place? Get enough sleep. Want to read social cues better so that you are a better teammate, friend, lover? Get enough sleep.

Chances are you don't get enough quality sleep, which may be the most important source of renewal that technology and social changes have conspired to rob from us. I'll explore it in depth in the chapter on physical resilience, but sleep also affects your mental, social, and spiritual well-being.

Deep disconnection—having little or no sense of belonging *just as you are*—makes isolation, physical pain, and meaninglessness feel permanent or intolerable. Trapped in the perpetual stress of fearing stress, while disconnected from sources of renewal, we become increasingly reluctant to take on the challenges that we need to stay strong, grow, and bounce back after adversity.

> Every one of the social and psychological causes of depression and anxiety . . . has something in common. They are all forms of disconnection. They are all ways in which we have been cut off from something we innately need but seem to have lost along the way.[3]
>
> —JOHANN HARI

We tolerate disconnection because it can yield a certain success—*for a while*. Compromising social and family life, workouts, and values allows us to work long hours, make more money, and get promoted, gaining power and prestige. This doesn't end well. Eventually, life presents difficulties that cannot be solved with money or power (although they enable formidable distractions).

Past generations had more opportunities for renewal, rebuilding, and growth built into daily life. Shared meals, entertainment, and work were the norm. Long commutes were impractical, schools and jobs were local, so people typically worked and went to school with friends and neighbors. Less automation and more expensive energy demanded more activity. Processed and junk food were less available. Churches and social clubs, now starving for members, were part of the majority's lives, solidifying community connections. Telling just one friend of difficulties could more easily activate a support network, because you and your friends were likely to share strong social connections.

Disconnection makes it easier to ignore others' troubles, treat others less humanely, or blame them for our own troubles. Although some would argue that this reflects independence, it is alienation and disconnection.

We have the most powerful information-sharing system in history, the internet. However, our negative bias is at home there;

much of what we share and read is shocking news, gossip, and posturing, poisonous to healthy relationships. Advertisers and some journalists fuel outrage because it leads to engagement with their messages.

> Research shows that the same content in an email and in in-person dialogue sounds less polite in the email.[4]
>
> —AMIT SOOD

Social media, rather than helping with loneliness, seems to make it worse. The more lonely people are, the more they use the internet, which then leads to greater loneliness, a 2013 survey of college students revealed.[5] Another survey showed that those who were lonely were more satisfied with their internet friends—but they were also more likely to say that their internet use was causing disturbances in their daily functioning.[6] A broad survey of internet users in 2018 showed that, contrary to concerns, Americans do become less lonely as they age. Yet those who reported overuse of social media—people who were worried that time spent on the internet was robbing them of in-person socializing—were lonelier.[7]

We face new threats—global terrorism, mass shootings, job insecurity, enormous debt, climate change, pandemics. Institutions—political, religious, academic, media—have lost much of their trust and authority. Greed, extremism, and scandals have created a void of wisdom, meaning, values, morality, and purpose. Few cultural leaders have hesitated to capitalize on fear, amplifying our stress reactions and feeding the vicious cycle of disconnection.

Threatened by modern fears, adrift and uninspired, we naturally react with the stress-driven behaviors of fight or flight, defend or distance, and selfish or survivalist. Some fight by trying to become more self-sufficient, planning for apocalypse. Others flee via distractions and indulgences to mask worries and helplessness; illness, divorce, and bankruptcy too often result. While we keep fighting and fleeing, disconnection deepens. Our hunger for connection shows up as compulsive texting while driving, overuse of social media, tribal politics, binary thinking, and rising rates of pain-masking addictions.

We don't need constant negative messages. We are wired for negativity. Far more than we need to be reminded of what to fear, we need to remember what's good in life.

- We are not likely to forget that we sometimes must fear or distrust strangers. We need to know, thoroughly and intuitively, that although some people will neglect, reject, and hurt us, we are not alone. We need to care and be cared for.
- We are unlikely to forget that the universe has diseases and dangers that can injure and kill us. We need to know, thoroughly and intuitively, that the physical world is our home, nourishing and sustaining us. We are creation's beneficiaries and stewards.
- Few of us will forget that we are far from perfect. We need to know, thoroughly and intuitively, that we are accepted just as we are, one body of humanity even as we are individuals.

In this environment, calls for "trigger warnings" (which research suggests are unhelpful, especially in the absence of clinical illness[8]) and bans on "microaggression" are not surprising. If you see stress as a problem to avoid, it makes sense to hold others responsible for causing it. But your difficulty probably has far less to do with other people's behavior and is more the result of your disconnection from sources of renewal, healing, and growth.

A culture of avoiding stress weakens everyone. "Stress-free living" is an oxymoron. When we advocate the goal of eliminating stress, we should not be surprised at the rise in addictions, distractions, and the ultimate "stress reduction"—suicide, which has risen 24 percent in the last five years.

To thrive in the twenty-first century, we must be more intentional about connection and renewal from stress than our ancestors were. We need to discern what truly threatens us and what does not, replacing the vicious cycle of fear, distraction, and disconnection with a virtuous cycle of connection and renewal.

It would be unfair to make these observations without acknowledging that racism, discrimination, circumstances, and privilege result in uneven opportunities to nurture the kinds of connections that build resilience. If you are struggling for basic survival, resilience routines may seem out of reach. If you are working multiple jobs just to make enough to pay the rent, eating well, and getting exercise and enough sleep may be impossible. That's realism. But resilience also calls for optimism, to have faith that even though the way forward individually may be bleak, great transformation happens when many of us take small steps forward.

Resilience routines are antidotes to fear-based thinking and acting because they nourish and strengthen you in body, mind, and spirit. They can help you heal from the past, cope with the present, and prepare for a better future.

building strength and resilience

Many kinds of stress and renewal habits make you stronger and more resilient. You already naturally do some of them. The ones you'll find in chapters 5–7 are backed by scientific evidence and informed by my education and experiences—personal growth, professional training, and many years of practice in crisis intervention and peer support.

I have provided references to many research papers, aiming whenever possible to cite meta-analyses and reviews that evaluate and summarize bodies of research. Some of these papers surely will be eventually revised or even discredited—self-correction is how science moves forward. If you dive into the research, perhaps the most important caution to keep in mind is that correlation does not mean causation: the fact that two things tend to happen together does not mean that one is causing the other. Researchers frequently observe correlations, but identifying causes is much harder, especially in systems as complex as human beings and societies. To illustrate this, consider why dogs become increasingly aggressive toward mail carriers and other delivery people. The carrier approaches a house and the dog barks. The carrier leaves, immediately. In the dog's brain, the carrier's departure is a signal that barking worked, because the dog has no idea that the carrier is simply headed for the next house. Keep repeating this pattern and the dog becomes "confident" that aggression drives away delivery people—because, to a dog, correlation always means causation. Don't make the same mistake as you read about scientific research.

Here is what science reveals. The stress and renewal of building and maintaining relationships with things, people, and wisdom generates strength to thrive and bounce back after adversity. Deeply engage with the material world that nourishes you, with communities that support you, and with values that give your life meaning and purpose. Remember, you can't fool your autopilot into "knowing" something you have not experienced. Become open to new experiences. As some wise person once said, "Nothing changes if nothing changes."

Growing more optimistic and realistic is challenging. It's not easy to let go of the refuges of denial, perfectionism, expectations, resentments, bitterness, and judgment. It takes courage to accept yourself and the world as they are; courage requires vulnerability. You'll need to believe, even if you feel stuck, that your intelligence and personality can change.

As you'll read in later chapters, physical resilience is primarily about using and caring for things—your body and nature. Mental resilience is about information and strategy—managing independence and privacy while collaborating and sharing with others. Spiritual resilience is about responsibility—managing the balance between caring for yourself and caring for others. In each of these complicated areas of being human, our greatest gifts often also are our greatest weaknesses. Strong leaders can be overcontrolling; gifted thinkers can be all strategy with no action; inspirational people may ignore their own needs and give others unwanted "gifts" for the sake of appearances. One consequence of this complexity is that you are the only expert about your own life. Experienced people and experts can be your teachers and guides, but don't surrender your choices to any book or person.

Resilience routines are habits of choosing stress and renewal— the right kinds and amounts, at the right intervals.

New habits? I don't stick with new habits.

It's not about sticking with them. You won't. Nobody does, consistently. Here's the good news—you don't have to. Even Olympic athletes and Navy SEALs skip practice sometimes. But this book is neither for nor about exceptional people; it is for ordinary people in ordinary circumstances. If you forget, neglect, or decide to skip a day, *start over*. Try again. There is no deadline. This isn't work or school, so nobody is grading, except you—and judging yourself is a self-defeating habit. Have compassion for yourself. Practice being as kind to yourself as you would be with a struggling friend. Small successes become large ones over time. Give yourself unlimited permission to fail and start over. Be gentle with yourself.

Forming new habits is simple but not easy. Resist the temptation to try to do too much at once. Start small and increase slowly. Break down big tasks into smaller ones. Let these two instructions guide you: *start small, start over*. Building resilience requires willpower, motivation, impulse control, perspective, and flexibility . . . but those are in short supply when you aren't resilient! That's why "start small, start over" is essential. Just as you can temporarily lift too much weight in the gym, you can easily fool yourself into thinking you can make big changes rapidly. But you are almost certain to exhaust and probably injure yourself.

That you do something good for yourself regularly isn't proof of self-discipline and willpower. Here's an easy test: What happens if you must skip the activity? If you are a regular exerciser, what do you feel when you don't exercise? Relief? Or a struggle with anxiety that you *should not* have skipped it? If you attend church regularly but can't get there one day, do you wrestle with guilt? Persistent anxiety and guilt are signs of *inflexibility,* not willpower. When the part of your brain that provides motivation, impulse control, and self-discipline is in charge, you can do things you don't feel like doing because you know they are the right thing to do. Flexibility includes the power to go against your habits, even the good ones, when necessary.

Start small is also important because in this disconnected world, many of us are carrying a lot of old stress. When you are weighed down by accumulated stress, rebuilding your strength is like recovering from an orthopedic injury. You need the *right amount* of stress to restore your strength. Too little (or none) and you won't heal. Too much and you will reinjure yourself. Pay attention to your intuition, but also seek the wisdom of others who've either been there themselves or have a lot of experience coaching others back to strength. Step out of your comfort zone, but not too far. Increase the "weight" you lift—physical, social, or spiritual—gradually.

Set aside willpower and self-discipline as the source of habit building. Instead, just try to be more *consistent.* People who aim to smoke the same number of cigarettes a day are more successful at reduction than those who just try and quit. *Small* acts of self-control will slowly increase your willpower, but whatever you try and control through willpower is most likely to fail.

This book doesn't try to be a laundry list of all possible resilience routines. You don't need that. Instead, what follows are the best examples I can find of the types of routines that help people become and remain stronger and more resilient. I will mostly stick to what is practical. I aim to show you the big picture, so that you have a better understanding and appreciation for the *kinds* of habits that contribute to well-being, strength, and resilience. When you see a routine that sounds appealing, helpful, or even intimidating in a way that suggests it might make a positive difference, look for websites, books, coaches, or classes that will help you learn that type of routine in enough depth that you can practice it well.

Don't get carried away with one kind of resilience routine. For example, there's a lot of talk today about mindfulness, which is certainly a powerful practice, but it is just one part of resilience.

Staying connected to things, people, and values gives you access to resources to overcome obstacles and seize opportunities, but resources are only part of the story. Relationships matter a great deal because your stress autopilot goes by "seeing is believing." To prevent sticking, it needs regular experiences that show you *belong,* physically, socially, and spiritually. The stress autopilot, anxious about the past, worried about the future, comes up with all sorts of "if only" reasons that you are not worthy of belonging right now: if only I were in better shape, if only I stopped drinking, if only I get that promotion, if only I made more money . . . and so on.

Physical belonging means knowing you *belong to creation,* that the universe gave rise to you. This helps you tolerate physical pain and force, knowing that they are normal and temporary parts of life. It also means that creation belongs to us, not as owners but as stewards—caretakers of the earth and nature.

Social belonging means knowing we *belong to one another*— family, friends, clubs, teams, and other social institutions. This helps us tolerate the pain of isolation and know that it also is a normal and temporary part of life. Meaningful belonging is not based on social media–style boasting or agreement with others' politics, religion, or other beliefs. It comes from welcoming others into your life because they share similar struggles and triumphs at the core of what it means to be alive and human—grief, joy, shared struggles, failures, and accomplishments.

Spiritual belonging means knowing that you *belong to a higher power or purpose,* that the pain of meaninglessness is also normal and temporary.

As Brené Brown brilliantly observes, belonging is not the same as "fitting in." They are opposites. You can only know, deep in your heart and gut, that you truly *belong* when you can let go of whatever you are pretending to be in trying to please, control, or impress others. "This above all else," famously wrote Shakespeare in *Hamlet*. "To thine own self be true. And it must follow, as the night the day, thou canst not then be false to any man."

The desire to fit in will tempt you to act like someone you are not. You may find acceptance that way, but then who belongs? Not your true self. Meanwhile, projecting a false identity will consume your time and energy.

> Be Here.
> Be You.
> Belong.
>
> —BRENÉ BROWN

safe and healthy connection

The physical, social, and spiritual connections this book advocates aren't the same as unhealthy attachments driven by anxious, suspicious, or desperate craving. Exercise at the gym builds strength, but learn how to use weights, machines, and other equipment to avoid injury. Connecting with nature is a resilience routine, but don't go running off into the wilderness unprepared. Do not forget that nature is also a source of infectious viruses and bacteria, deadly storms, earthquakes, and dangerous animals.

Healthy social connections are dependable, but that doesn't mean they are irreplaceable. Hold on loosely. To avoid betrayal, take time to build trust. Have boundaries and realize that when you do, some people will criticize you for them under the mistaken impression that being resilient means you should tolerate abusive and toxic people. Social connection is not control. Military recruits are *connected* to their drill sergeant, but that kind of connection, which shuns emotion, comes to an end, often abruptly, when the relationship no longer serves its purpose.

Spiritual connection, shared values, and purposes are important, but beware of cults and fundamentalism in their religious, political, and other forms.

Generosity is powerful, but being generous doesn't mean being nice. It means being *kind*. When we are nice, it's usually so that other people will like us. When we are kind, the recipient cannot repay the debt. Similarly, gratitude is not just being polite. It means appreciating people and creation as gifts.

measuring stress and renewal reactions

There would be little point in promoting healthy rhythms of stress and renewal without evidence to support which ones are effective. Although research is far from complete, we are fortunate to live in a time when our ability to measure what's going on in our brains and bodies is expanding. New, faster, and less invasive sensors, faster computers, and innovations in software analysis are opening the doors to more and better objective measures of stress and renewal.

As the tale of the two wolves illustrated, your stress and renewal reactions are two sides of your autonomic nervous system—the sympathetic, which responds to stress, and the parasympathetic, which activates renewal. The two branches have associated hormones, which also send signals throughout your system. When you have a stress response, researchers want to know how strong it is and to distinguish between the challenge and threat responses discussed earlier. They also want objective measures of your flexibility—how quickly the stress response subsides and renewal activators kick in.

STRESS RESPONSE SIGNS

Heart rate and blood pressure are two of most easily measured signs of a stress reaction. Challenge and threat responses raise your heart rate, but only a threat response increases your blood pressure. Other simple measurements include the other components of polygraph "lie detectors"—respiration rate and sweat, measured by the electrical conductivity of skin.

The three primary stress hormones are adrenaline (also called epinephrine), noradrenaline (also called norepinephrine), and cortisol. They have similar effects: they get you ready for action by increasing your heart's output and delivering more fuel— sugar and oxygen—to your brain and muscles. Adrenaline and noradrenaline are fast acting, while cortisol's effect takes longer but is more persistent. Noradrenaline increases your focus and alertness.

When researchers want to see the effect of stress or renewal-inducing experiences, they may measure adrenaline, cortisol, or related protein or enzyme levels in saliva, urine, blood, or cerebrospinal fluid (CSF). Of course, drawing blood is stressful and CSF even more so, which can confound research, so saliva is more often used. Saliva is part of your immune system, a first-line defense against microorganisms. Stress hampers your immune system when you don't experience sufficient renewal. To measure that effect, researchers sometimes look at salivary proteins, such as immunoglobulin A (IgA) and chromogranin C (CgA), and an enzyme, alpha-amylase, to measure immune system strength.[9]

Outside of sports medicine, there is relatively little research focused on measuring renewal. Studies often regard lowered stress markers alone as indicators of renewal. Especially in sports, however, research sometimes also looks at the biochemicals that send renewal signals to the brain and body, such as testosterone and other androgens, which help rebuild muscles after exercise. Other renewal hormones are oxytocin, vasopressin, growth hormone, and DHEA.

Oxytocin, sometimes dubbed the "love hormone," has received increasing attention in recent years, after researchers recognized its role in social bonding and trust. Although oxytocin was identified more than a hundred years ago, until recently it was seen only as a pregnancy hormone, often used to stimulate delivery. Researchers failed to notice its role in stress and renewal because until the mid-1990s they had excluded female subjects from most studies, out of concern that monthly hormone cycles would confound data interpretation. Although oxytocin is released during stress, it acts mainly to enhance renewal rather than to buffer stress.[10]

Analyzing the effect of stress and renewal hormones on the brain is challenging because taking measurements inside the brain is difficult or impossible, while levels in saliva, blood, and urine don't always correlate well to brain levels.[11] Measuring them in cerebrospinal fluid would be better, but the process is painful and unsuitable to continuous or frequent testing.

There's one more problem with measuring hormone levels—hormones only work if your body has enough working "receptors" for them to influence. If the hormones were groceries, measuring the number of trucks carrying them is only meaningful if there are enough stores ready to unload the food. If there are not, people will go hungry. "Insulin resistance" in type 2 diabetes is such a problem. Your pancreas produces enough insulin, but your cells can't utilize it properly, so measuring insulin levels is not useful. The same kind of problem has been shown to affect nearly all of the hormones this book describes. You can even end up with an "epi-genetic" receptor deficit, literally inheriting trauma from your ancestors.

I have wondered how much trauma I may have inherited. My maternal grandfather was one of the British Army soldiers who nearly starved to death during the horrible battle of Gallipoli during World War I. I'm told he destroyed all photos of himself from that time because he looked so emaciated. You'll find Grampa in the history of Alcoholics Anonymous as "Davey R.," the Scottish engineer from New Jersey who started more AA chapters than anyone throughout the southeastern United States. His sobriety came after my mother reached adulthood; he was a violent drunk when she was growing up. My father came out of a different kind of adversity. He was a sharecropper's son who grew up in the poverty of western Virginia and served as a gunner aboard light attack bombers, flying thirty-one missions over Germany during World War II. Dad went on to receive a PhD in philosophy from Columbia University and had a career teaching that subject. Along with their other challenges, my parents grew up during the Great Depression.

NERVOUS SYSTEM SIGNALS

Heart rate variability, or HRV, is a fascinating peek into your resilience. Here's how it works. As you inhale, your heart speeds up, and as you exhale, it slows down. The change is so small that you usually can't notice it. With sensitive heart rate monitors and computers, however, researchers have found that they can track HRV. People with high HRV (their hearts speed up and slow down more than average) are more resilient, physically and mentally. That's not surprising, since the things we know make people resilient—being in good physical condition, getting enough sleep, having strong social support and the other attitudes and activities we've discussed—all contribute to higher HRV. You might also think of it as having a *flexible* heart rate, one that doesn't easily get stuck in a stress response.

Here's the surprise. Using a biofeedback device to increase your HRV also makes you more resilient—physically and psychologically. Our minds and bodies are powerful enough that we can activate our parasympathetic nervous system (feed the good wolf) through biofeedback alone. A number of the recent research studies I have cited have used HRV as a primary measure of test subjects' renewal and resilience.

You can install HRV monitoring apps on your smartphone. They work in conjunction with heart rate sensors, but only those more sensitive ones that strap around your chest. The wrist-based ones don't capture data with enough precision.

I've been experimenting with HRV apps over the last year. Although the software is still a bit confusing and unreliable, I have been able to see some of the effects of my own resilience routines. I confess that the unreliability of the technology (flakey Bluetooth connections) has kept me from making a habit of doing the biofeedback part. Still, the technology has great promise. If you like gadgets (as I do), it is worth a try.

building your flexibility

Physical, social, and spiritual health and strength are important for everyone, so don't imagine that you can ignore any of the dimensions of resilience. To grow stronger and more flexible and resilient, each of us needs a different mixture of stress and renewal, which can change with the seasons of our lives. Identifying what you need, as you journey through life, requires self-awareness, which is why *noticing* is so powerful. Consider this chapter an invitation to get to know yourself better—which means letting go of the assumption that you already know everything about yourself that you need to. Progress requires ongoing self-reflection.

> The unexamined life is not worth living.
>
> **—SOCRATES**

But wait a moment. Before we explore *new* resilience routines that could benefit you, consider this important question: *What has worked for you in the past?* You know yourself better than anyone. Think back to opportunities you seized, challenges you overcame, or difficulties that you got through. What helped you? This exercise will also help you gain insight for the next section of this chapter.

Who in your life has been truly supportive, standing beside you through a challenging or difficult time? Write down their names.[1]

What did you do that helped quiet an excessive stress response—anxiety, difficult thoughts and feelings—or helped you to accomplish a goal? Was there a song that you played repeatedly? Did you go for walks? Get a massage? Write these down.

What wisdom did you hear, read, or recall that was enlightening or comforting? Was there a book, song lyrics, quote, or memory that helped? Write these down too.

Now that you have written down things that helped in the past, describe an opportunity, challenge, or difficulty you are facing now. Look through what helped in the past and consider what will be helpful now. Write a resilience plan for your present situation, using the past resources as a guide. When you decide the order for carrying it out, get out of your comfort zone—but not far. Just like at the gym, starting small helps avoid the failure of overdoing it.

You can learn more from this exercise by debriefing with yourself when you are done. What worked? Which resources helped the most and why? Which were the least helpful and why? Did you recognize resources to add to your list? Consider applying what you have learned to other areas of your life—other opportunities, challenges, or difficulties.

choosing new routines: when is your greatest gift an obstacle?

The most difficult part of knowing which new resilience routines will most benefit you is this: your greatest gift becomes an obstacle when you overuse it as a strategy to *fit in* rather than cultivating connections where you *belong* as your true self. As we grow and develop into adults, we build habits—gifts—that help each of us adapt to the unique stresses of our circumstances. That adaptation shows the amazing flexibility of humans. Yet if you don't learn how and when to "turn off" the primary gift of your childhood, it leads to disconnection more than belonging.

The gift in fight or flight is *power*. It triggers changes to your body that help you rise to physical challenges and threats— acquiring, enhancing, defending, owning, and using things, in- cluding your body, finances, tools, and other possessions. This gift becomes a liability when you have trouble seeing life as anything other than a battle. Although having power can satisfy your stress autopilot's desire for *control*, it becomes disconnecting when you are not the one in charge.

The gift in defend and distance is *empathy*. It helps you rise to the mental and emotional challenges and threats of dealing with people without becoming overwhelmed: enemies, competitors, teachers, coaches, mentors, family, communities, tribes—living, working, competing, cooperating, and playing with others. When you overuse the gift of defend and distance, you care too much about what other people think of you. Although empathy satisfies your stress autopi- lot's desire for *companionship*, it becomes disconnecting when you need to say no to others and pursue your own goals.

The gift in selfish and survivalist is *safety*. It urges you to focus on being prepared to meet immediate rather than long-term needs; looking out for yourself and those you care most about. This gift becomes a liability when you care so much about strat- egy and planning that you don't get around to acting on your knowledge. Although preparedness satisfies your stress autopilot's desire for *predictability*, it becomes disconnecting when you need to *act* rather than gather knowledge and develop strategy.

Building resilience does not mean abandoning your gifts. It is okay to take control sometimes, okay to be concerned about your image sometimes, and okay to spend some energy preparing for possibilities. Building resilience means expanding your tool kit, allowing you to respond to life with greater flexibility by strength- ening the areas where you are weaker, not by weakening yourself where you are strong.

Now we will dive deeper into the three categories of gifts/ weaknesses by mapping them to the Enneagram, an ancient tool for gaining insight into personality development. If you tend to stay stuck in fight or flight, your gift/weakness is *power,* and you may be a Challenger, Mediator, or Reformer. If you tend to defend or distance, your gift/weakness is *empathy,* and you may be a Helper, Achiever, or Romantic. If your sticking place is selfish and survivalist, your gift/weakness is *safety,* and you may be an Observer, Questioner, or Enthusiast.

For better or worse, much has been written and (unfortunately) argued about the Enneagram in recent years. The personality types are generalizations; use them wisely. Nobody is entirely one type, so don't assume that just because something feels familiar, it defines you. Give it space and time to sink in. This is food for thought, hopefully leading to a few "aha" moments, much more diagnostic and descriptive than prescriptive. Used wisely, the Enneagram can help you to gain some insight into parts of yourself that are difficult to see. The personality types are certainly not rigid categories with sharp dividing lines or boxes that you cannot escape.

- Challengers, Mediators, and Reformers undermine their resilience by habitually treating life as a fight-or-flight battle. Anger—the stress autopilot's reaction to the present—underlies these types. If this is you, you are quick to say no and hold your own opinions tightly. You need to build strength to let go of idealism, to nurture mercy and unconditional love, and have the grace to accept progress rather than demanding perfection.

  - Difficulty belonging: When you are not leading.
  - Primary renewal need: Physical—rest and digest.

- Helpers, Achievers, or Romantics undermine their resilience by habitually treating life as a chore of avoiding rejection. Anxiety—the stress autopilot's reaction to the past—underlies these types. If this is you, you take too much responsibility, hold too tightly to appearances, planning how to impress others and solve problems that are not your own. Resign as general manager of the universe!

- Difficulty belonging: When it feels like you have nothing to give.
- Primary renewal need: Spiritual—pause and plan.

■ Observers, Questioners, and Enthusiasts undermine their resilience by habitually treating life as a selfish and survivalist concern for their own safety. Worry—the stress autopilot's fears about the future—underlies these types. If this is you, you tend to isolate, holding too tightly to your thoughts and imagination. To become more flexible, become less detached, engage, transforming information into wisdom, strategy into action.

- Difficulty belonging: When you have to rely on others.
- Primary renewal need: Social—tend and befriend.

ANGRY AND STUCK IN FIGHT: "MY WAY OR THE HIGHWAY" CHALLENGERS[2]

If you overuse the Challenger's gift, others will see you as controlling, insensitive, blunt, domineering, and aggressive. Challengers act as though they cannot *belong* unless they are in control. Clues that this is your gift include a love of competition, impatience with incompetence, annoyance when you stick your neck out for others but they don't appreciate it, difficulty letting go of injustices, and putting a lot of pressure on yourself. Your idea of *fitting in* is for people to behave properly. You may become angry when they don't follow the rules, which isolates you when you can't let go of their transgressions.

If you are a Challenger, you will grow the most by increasing your social stress and renewal, which will help you to stay in the moment while keeping your opinions and judgments to yourself. You will learn to take your stress autopilot's desire for control less seriously. Develop your empathy by giving more attention to others' points of view. Become more willing to compromise for the sake of relationships. Practice mercy.

Spiritual engagement will also benefit you, helping you to let go of your high expectations. If you are religious, the phrase "Let go and let God" will help.

ANGRY AND STUCK IN FLIGHT: LAZY, INDECISIVE MEDIATORS[3]

If you are a Mediator, you seek harmony and act as if it is impossible to *belong* while in conflict. Your tendency to distance yourself urges you to attempt to *fit in* by keeping a low profile, which others may mistake for peacefulness. You are willing to defend, but only on behalf of others, to end conflict, but your failure to address your own needs isolates you. "Go along and get along" might be your motto. Overusing this gift can leave you with difficulty making decisions because you see all sides. You are so attuned to others' needs and wants that you may not even be aware of your own.

A Mediator's primary gift is physically stressful, so make sure you are getting the rest and digest you need. Mind-body exercises such as martial arts, yoga, and Pilates will help you to become more aware of what's going on within yourself.

You will grow the most by increasing spiritual stress and renewal. Become more decisive by wrestling with values and priorities. Develop trust in your own point of view, a stronger sense of right and wrong, so that when making a choice matters, you can commit. You will learn to take your stress autopilot's urge to "check out" less seriously.

You also need more social engagement. Others may enjoy your company, but if that is because you are so accommodating, they aren't taking you seriously. Learn to pay less attention to others' problems while investing more in noticing and sharing your thoughts and reactions. You'll discover that you have anger and resentments that will lose their power when you vent them safely with trusted companions.

ANGRY AND STUCK IN FIGHT AND FLIGHT: "NOTHING IS GOOD ENOUGH" REFORMERS

Reformers,[4] who have the gift of perfectionism, struggle to accept themselves and others as they are. If you are a Reformer, you have high standards and attention to detail. You may appear self-disciplined, but your love of control makes you rigid, demanding, and critical. You act as if you won't *belong* unless things are exactly as you imagine they should be. You try to *fit in* by being perfect, but your own failures end up isolating you.

A Reformer's primary gift is physically stressful, so make sure you are taking breaks and getting the rest and digest you need. Know that it is okay to relax sometimes. You need tranquility and serenity; calming physical renewal will benefit you greatly, helping you to accept life rather than constantly reacting to it.

You are out of touch with yourself and your values, so you will benefit from increasing both social and spiritual engagement. You will learn to ignore or even sometimes silence your stress autopilot's perfectionism. As you struggle with acceptance, you will learn to stop focusing on how everything *should* be and stop trying to fix yourself and other people.

"Don't criticize," a motto of Codependents Anonymous, will help you to let go of the need to impose your perfectionism on others. Become more "selfish" by turning your "shoulds" into "wants," which will lower your guilt and shame. Reflect on your priorities and learn not to take yourself quite so seriously. Laugh at yourself. Figure out what *you* need and learn to ask for it. Try out these mottos: "Eighty percent is perfect" and "Done is better than good."

ANXIOUS AND STUCK IN DEFENDING: PROUD, PUSHY, ATTENTION-SEEKING HELPERS[5]

The gift of helpfulness becomes a liability when you need to be needed, trying to *fit in* by *earning* acceptance or love. Helpers act as if they won't *belong* if they say no to others. Tired of lifting other people's weights? Worry that you might be too selfish? If these sound familiar and you are sensitive to criticism and disapproval, you may be overusing the gift of helpfulness. Your focus on helping others distances you from everyone, including yourself. Your helpfulness, while admirable, is more about getting other people to need, like, and approve of you than a true spirit of generosity. Ask yourself, "What is my intent?"

As a Helper, you naturally take on a lot of social stress, so ensure that you are taking breaks and getting plenty of tend and befriend social renewal.

Helpers become more flexible and resilient by adding spiritual stress and renewal, which will help to reset your priorities. Seek humility rather than investing so much energy into rescuing and people pleasing. You need self-compassion along with your empathy for everyone's feelings. Like a Reformer, you need to make yourself more of a priority, but in your case pause and plan will help you learn when to say no.

You're so busy caring for others, you also need to step up your physical stress and renewal—exercise, sleep, diet, nature, and so on.

ANXIOUS AND STUCK IN DISTANCING: PRAISE-HUNGRY, LYING TASKMASTER ACHIEVERS[6]

Like Helpers, Achievers are motivated by the image they present to others, acting as if others don't admire what they do, they won't *belong*. Achievers try to *fit in* by pointing out their accomplishments and are quite tempted to lie about them. They discover that admiration is a cheap substitute for acceptance and love. If you follow the Achiever pattern, instead of acting like a human *being*, you spend most of your time as a human *doing*.

Achievers, like Helpers and Romantics, take on the exhausting daily task of figuring out what will appeal to others. Ensure that you are taking breaks and getting the physical renewal you need.

As an Achiever, you'll gain the most from adding social stress and renewal. Being real with others will be difficult; true social connection relies on vulnerability and acceptance, not boasting. Spiritual engagement also benefits Achievers. To shift your priorities toward yourself and build integrity, you need to resist the temptation to lie about your failures and accomplishments.

ANXIOUS AND STUCK IN DEFENDING AND DISTANCING: ENVIOUS, "I'M SPECIAL" ROMANTICS[7]

Like Helpers and Achievers, Romantics are motivated primarily by the image they present to the world. If this is you, you act as though you won't *belong* unless others see you as special. Romantics (also called Individualists or Artists) try to *fit in* by using imagination to draw others in, seeking deep emotional connection. They tend to compare themselves to others and take things personally. They confuse longing for connection for actually having it. In their quest to be one of a kind, Romantics struggle with idealism, simplicity, and authenticity.

Like the other anxious types, you are at risk of being physically worn out by your efforts. Make sure you take breaks and experience physical renewal.

Romantics increase flexibility and resilience by adding equal doses of physical and social engagement. Physical engagement will help you become more grounded, practical, and positive. Social engagement will address your need to connect with others more meaningfully and become less self-absorbed. Learn to listen to others without becoming enmeshed. Becoming a detached observer of yourself and others will help you connect more deeply. Broadening your social support network is important. Keep things simple.

WORRIED AND STUCK IN SELFISH: GREEDY, OVER-THINKING OBSERVERS[8]

The Observer seeks safety in knowledge yet often is detached and lost in preparedness strategies. If you are an Observer, you act as if appearing foolish or depending on others for information means you don't *belong*. Observers may attempt to *fit in* by unreasonably dominating a conversation to desperately prove that they know something.

As a worrier, your primary need for renewal is spiritual. Take breaks to pause and plan, and seek inspiration and a sense of awe and wonder.

Physical stress and renewal will make Observers more flexible and resilient by building habits of taking action and trusting instincts. You will learn to take your stress autopilot's demand to know everything less seriously. To get out of your head, you also need to be quicker to speak up and stand up for yourself even when you might be wrong, so social engagement will also help.

WORRIED AND STUCK IN SURVIVAL: FEARFUL, OVER-PREPARED QUESTIONERS[9]

To the Questioner, safety comes from rules and authority. If you are a Questioner (also called a Trooper or Devil's Advocate), you seek certainty and predictability. You act as though you won't *belong* if you are caught off guard. You are often living in the future, considering possibilities and worst-case scenarios more than probabilities. You may attempt to *fit in* by acting tough, as though you are prepared for everything. You are likely to spread yourself too thin, trying to prepare for so many different possibilities that you are not truly ready for any of them. "That's the way we've always done it" appeals to you, yet you also want to keep all of your options open.

As another worrier, you also have a high need for spiritual renewal, but when you take a break from your worries, pausing is much more important than planning. Consider priorities rather than possibilities. Pausing and planning can help you to become more objective.

If you are a Questioner, increasing your physical stress and renewal will help ground you in the present and reduce worrying about how you will survive the future. Learn to trust your instincts and be able to act with incomplete information.

WORRIED AND STUCK IN SELFISH AND SURVIVALIST: STIMULATION-SEEKING, GLUTTONOUS ENTHUSIASTS[10]

Enthusiasts don't like it when someone rains on their parade or is a party pooper. Enthusiasts act as though showing pain or sorrow will mean they don't *belong*. In contrast to the narrow perspective of the Questioner, the Enthusiast often ignores details in favor of seeing the big picture. If you are an Enthusiast, you are easily bored and often seek fulfillment in stimulating experiences—travel, parties, and so on. You dream of adventures, but they often remain little more than dreams. Your motto might be "More!" Seeking to avoid pain, you have a hard time being serious and are at risk for addiction to substances. You attempt to *fit in* by acting as if optimism and positive thinking will solve every problem, but that isolates you from people who are suffering.

As the third type of worrier, you also have a high need for spiritual renewal to balance your optimism with a healthy measure of realism. Make sure that you are taking breaks to pause and plan to work on your sense of perspective.

Enthusiasts become more flexible and resilient by adding more social and spiritual engagement. Social stress and renewal will help you learn to observe your pain and indecisiveness without judging them and to become more interested in the welfare of others and less interested in pleasing yourself. The perspective that spiritual stress and renewal build will help you learn to take only what you need.

physical resilience routines: connecting to things

A s a way to help remember the dimension of stress and renewal, I have borrowed a motto from firefighting, in which we frequently scan above, around, or under us: "Look up, look down, look around."

Look down is the *physical* reminder. When you look down, you see your own body and the earth. This includes other material resources to be grateful for, such as food, shelter, and money. In exchange, we need to be good stewards of the resources we own and use. Physical routines connect you with your body, material objects, the earth, and living things. These include getting what you need through diet, exercise, sleep, training, tools, and finances and being generous with your time, talents, and possessions.

Look down *is* the reminder to stay connected to the material world. Little else matters when you don't feel physically safe and strong. These routines are about building your *power*, especially the power to say no to distractions and temptations. They keep you connected with *things*—nature, your body, tools, "muscle memory," finances—for nourishment, shelter, health, skills, strength, and so forth. Your stress autopilot wants to know that you have resources to protect yourself and those you care about from physical threats: injury, illness, bankruptcy, unemployment, homelessness, theft, and so forth.

Adding more physical engagement (stress and renewal) is most important if you are an Observer, Questioner, or Enthusiast. You tend to spend a lot of time in your head; learning to take action will help you to become more resilient and flexible.

Challengers, Peacemakers, and Reformers are often physically engaged but not in a healthy way, using force to control and dominate. If you are one of these, more rest and digest will help you become flexible about backing down.

Even though you may have learned to ignore your body's warnings, your stress autopilot still knows, through nerves, hormones, and other biological messaging, if you are rested, fed, strong, skilled, and healthy. If it does not regularly receive those signals, it is more likely to set off a threat response or to stay stuck there. Physical habits also help you avoid the chronic stress of worrying about or having illnesses associated with inactivity, insomnia, obesity, poor nutrition, and so forth. Your autopilot also is aware of how *dependable* your physical resources are. If your income is unreliable or expenses are out of control, if your housing or meals are uncertain, you aren't getting enough deep sleep, or you are not confident about important physical skills, such as driving, your autopilot raises your alert level.

Building financial and material strength is like building your muscles—the "exercise" itself is stressful, but you'll end up better off. Most of us have a good idea of what it means to get in shape physically. You exercise, stressing your muscles, then give them time and nourishment to renew and grow. The pattern of *stress, renewal, repeat* applies to all resilience routines, not just physical ones.

If you have experienced trauma—and virtually everyone will, at some point in their lives—physical resilience routines, especially renewal, are essential because of the physical stickiness of stress reactions. Bessel van der Kolk, author of the wonderful best seller *The Body Keeps the Score*, writes, "In order to change, people need to become aware of their sensations and the way that their bodies interact with the world around them. Physical self-awareness is the first step in releasing the tyranny of the past." In other words, *noticing* what's going on in your body is a foundation of physical renewal routines.

Unlike social or spiritual assets, you can objectively measure many kinds of physical stress. You can track calories, steps, how far you run, how much you lift, how you get and spend money, your blood pressure, heart rate, oxygen, and sugar levels. With modern technology, you can even monitor your sleep quality at home. Measurement and tracking are nearly always good, especially when they help you maintain a long-term perspective rather than focusing on the ups and downs that always are part of progress.

ROUTINE: WORKING OUT—CHOOSING THE STRESS OF PHYSICAL EXERCISE

Although rest is essential to build strength, too much resting, just like too much stress, is bad for you. Physical inactivity is associated with increased risk for at least thirty-five diseases and disorders, including the top ten leading causes of death in the United States.[1] Inactivity contributes to cancers, type 2 diabetes, high cholesterol, high blood pressure, immune deficiencies, depression, dementia, osteoporosis, obesity, oxidative stress (molecular damage that contributes to many illnesses), and progressive loss of muscle mass and strength (sarcopenia).[2] Inactivity is expensive—the related health-care costs were estimated at close to $60 billion annually in 2016.[3]

To get an idea of how modern living has reduced our activity, researchers studied an Old Order Amish community in Canada, a farming community where cars, electric appliances, and other labor-saving devices are not in use. Obesity is almost nonexistent. Men walked more eighteen thousand steps a day and women walked more than fourteen thousand.

The usual target for healthy adults is to take ten thousand steps a day, which means that even our *goals* are well below the amount of exercise many of our ancestors undoubtedly got. The 2010 America on the Move study reported that the average person in the United States was taking little more than five thousand steps a day.[4]

Regular exercise combined with renewal and nourishment has multiple benefits. For example, your skeletal muscles are important for more than just movement. They are part of your endocrine system,[5] interacting with your pituitary, thyroid, and pancreas, which release hormones that regulate your health and response to injuries and illness.

- Even though stress hormones rise during exercise, regular workouts lower their resting levels and reduce your stress autopilot's sensitivity and stickiness, keeping hormone levels from spiking as high when you feel stress. As a result, exercise can lower your resting heart rate and blood pressure, while keeping them from rising as high when you react to stress, and helping them to return to their resting levels faster.
- As your muscles grow, your blood vessels also enlarge, reducing your odds of heart attack or stroke.[6]
- More muscle mass means that your body will consume glucose faster, reducing your blood sugar, helping you avoid or manage type 2 diabetes, while reducing inflammation.[7] High-intensity exercise is especially effective.[8]
- Exercise improves the functioning of cellular energy generators (mitochondria), reducing release of damaging oxidants.[9]
- Larger muscles create a larger reservoir for amino acids needed by the rest of your body.[10]
- Physical activity sends signals (myokines) that help regulate metabolism, inflammation,[11] and many other processes, including depression.[12] Exercise-induced myokines reduce belly fat.[13]

- Exercise "turns on" genes in the brain that reduce depression and increase resilience.[14]
- A survey of research on strength training mental health effects in adults showed that it can reduce anxiety, pain intensity from the lower back, osteoarthritis, and fibromyalgia, while reducing depression and improving sleep quality, cognition, and self-esteem.[15]

Don't overdo it. Extreme exercise, not giving yourself renewal time, or incurring a serious injury can increase your stress reactions instead of dampening them. In some studies, cardio or aerobic exercise appeared to be slightly more beneficial than weight training, but both help us become more resilient. Exercise needs to be consistent—the anti-inflammatory benefits of exercise vanish within a few days.

ROUTINE: MANAGING FINANCES AND POSSESSIONS

Well-being doesn't come from having more things—money, cars, houses, and the other common measures of success. It depends on managing them well. Having too much or too little can threaten your health and safety. Having too much—particularly if you become strongly attached to your things—can add a burden of management and care that detracts from the rest of your life. Recall that the more you care, the more stress you will feel when a thing you care about is threatened, damaged, or lost. Things are impermanent; many are frequently threatened and easy to lose. Not everyone becomes happier after such financial windfalls as winning the lottery.

Owning and owing can be stressful. Owing often leads to worrying about being able to repay. Owning can be stressful because the things we own may require skills to use, and they often require regular management or care. Owning and owing are not necessarily bad for you, but balance is key. Owe nothing and own nothing and you lack material resources. Owing too much or owning too much can consume your time and attention.

Owing too much is a frequent problem in the modern world. U.S. consumer debt reached a hard-to-grasp $13 *trillion* in 2018. Here's a breakdown:

- Credit cards: $834 billion (an all-time high).
- Mortgages: $9.4 trillion (also an all-time high).
- Personal loans: $291 billion, growing fastest.
- Student loans: $1.37 trillion (all-time high).
- Auto loans: $1.27 billion (all-time high).

The average U.S. household is nearly $140,000 in debt, even though the median income is less than $60,000, which means that many of us are living beyond our means. Unmanageable debt is a recipe for chronic stress, a marathon rather than the series of "sprints" of making monthly payments you are confident you can afford.

Debt impacts resilience in two ways. First, it creates uncertainty about our ability to have the essentials—food, shelter, and other necessities. Unless you've freely taken a vow of poverty, living a few paychecks away from homelessness generates constant stress. And remember that while there's nothing wrong with stress itself, *unrelieved* stress will wear you down. Whether you are thinking about your finances consciously or not, your stress autopilot will activate in response to financial uncertainty and unpredictability.

Debt also affects the important resilience traits of gratitude and generosity. It's hard to give a gift or donation when you aren't confident that you will be able to pay bills or save for retirement. It is hard to be grateful for money that only pays down debt.

Higher unsecured personal debt—credit cards and the like—has been linked to poorer health, especially depression, substance abuse, and suicide. Although research is limited and short term, the relationship between debt and health, both physical and mental, is clear from multiple studies.[16] Long-term research is needed to determine which one causes the other. In young people, high

personal debt correlates to crime, low self-esteem, social dysfunction, and feeling out of control of life,[17] a big stress autopilot
activator.

Although there are many money management approaches, I'm
going to describe the one that I learned from my financial mentor,
John Lemons, who was the initial outside investor in my first
start-up. John has been CEO of several Silicon Valley companies
and a protégé of Teledyne's Henry Singleton, widely regarded as
an excellent business leader. Singleton taught John, and John
taught me, that the key to managing finances is to focus on *cash
flow.*

We rarely end up in trouble because of bad ideas or plans, John
taught me. Trouble takes us by surprise when we don't forecast
cash flow, because by the time we can't pay our bills, it's too late.

For me, cash flow forecasting is like the overdue library book
nightmare. I don't want to think about what lies at the end—the
day the "lights go out" and we run out of money. For many business start-ups, until you grow revenue, that day is often just a few
months away (which is why we need investors).

Confession: I still hate to look at cash flow forecasts. My wife
does it for our household and she does it well. I'm grateful, even
though I still don't like looking at it.

Having more things than we need for the life we want weighs
us down. The $38 billion self-storage industry is growing rapidly,
as people accumulate stuff they don't have room for. Decluttering
and organizing services are growing rapidly, promoting themselves, accurately, as stress and anxiety reduction.

The more stuff you have and the less organized it is, the more
out of control it feels, an autopilot activator. Research shows that
people who describe their homes as cluttered are more depressed.

Marie Kondo has created a hit television series, *Tidying Up,* on
this topic. Here are her six rules:

1. Commit.
2. Imagine the ideal life you wish to live.

3. Discard first.
4. Tidy by category.
5. Follow the order above.
6. Ask yourself, "Does it spark joy?"

Purging accumulated stuff is a grief response I've seen in others and felt myself.

As I write this, I have a big container of screws, nails, and other fasteners, mostly left over from a remodeling project we had to abandon when the mortgage meltdown put our house far underwater (we bought at the *worst* possible time, November 2007). I know that my big box of fasteners wouldn't cost me a lot to replace, but I've had a terrible time letting go of it. I talk about the importance of generosity, but there's part of me that says I'm wasting money if I give them away.

Besides, I might need them someday. Sadly, that's the excuse for all sorts of stuff in drawers, closets, sheds, and shelves—so much that, more than once, I've bought something new because I forgot I already had one. I admit that I'm probably too attached to things, while living too much in the future, too much in *possible* futures. This kind of "possibility thinking" about unlikely events is a stress reaction.

Our relationships with things may not be all that different from our relationships with people. The social bonding hormone oxytocin responds to brand affiliations in much the same way as to social connections, researchers have found. It seems possible that falling in love—or at least having a deep bond—with a brand is more than just a metaphor![18]

ROUTINE: FOCUSED-ATTENTION MEDITATION

Are you distracted more easily than you'd like? Your brain has an "attention network" that helps you stay focused on a task. You can improve it through "focused-attention meditation." You practice giving your full, undivided attention to one thing, notice when your mind wanders, then refocus on it. The most common thing to focus on is your breathing. Unlike relaxing, letting-go and focused-attention forms of meditation take effort, especially when you are a beginner.

If you notice that your mind keeps drifting, you might be tempted to think that you are meditating poorly. But *noticing* is the very skill this type of meditation develops—you develop more awareness of when your mind has drifted. You cannot deliberately return to the present until you notice that your mind has gone elsewhere. Practicing this type of meditation "badly" rewires your brain to stay present rather than experiencing anxiety from the past or worry about the future.[19] The positive effects are immediate, persistent, and improve over time.[20] Here's how to do it.

- Set a timer for a few minutes, something that's just a bit outside of your comfort zone.
- Sit in a way in which you can be alert yet relaxed. Close your eyes if you wish. Notice your position and posture. Avoid becoming rigid. Relax and breathe normally.
- Begin noticing your breathing. Feel the sensation of air coming in and going out. Let go of other thoughts.
- When you notice that your mind has wandered away from paying attention to your breathing, gently return.
- To wrap up, take a few deep breaths, noticing them.

Doing this regularly will bring about measurable improvements to your brain's attention network, helping you stay on task more often when you want to.

ROUTINE: TAKING TIME OUT

Stuck stress reactions can make you restless, hungry, and busy, busy, busy. "Time-out" practices such as silence and fasting, although stressful, can help quiet those urges as you stop talking, eating, judging, and evaluating. Research supports the positive effects of these practices. They can help strengthen your immune system, control your diet, clarify your thinking, and contribute to your overall health. Earlier, I suggested treating your life as a series of sprints rather than as a marathon. Time-out practices are related: we benefit physically, mentally, and spiritually from periodic breaks from the marathon of regular eating, thinking, and judging. Remember, resilience is about flexibility. Temporarily refraining from talk, food, and judgmental thinking can free you to pay attention. Although it's a cliché, there's truth in the idea that these routines help you become better in touch with yourself, tapping into the power of *noticing* more.

shortcuts for activating physical renewal

BREATHE SLOWLY AND DEEPLY

Those are the first words under the "Tools for Coping" cards that our crisis intervention team hands out. Controlled breathing is a type of meditation, a shortcut to physical relaxation. When you take a deep breath and let it out slowly, good things happen in your body. Your vagus nerve, the mind-body information highway, becomes more active, putting you more in touch with the present, less anxious about the past or worried about the future. Increased vagus nerve activity goes together with increased resilience. (Search online and you'll find quite a few books that focus entirely on methods of activating your vagus nerve.)

When your autopilot activates, you will tend to take shallow breaths, from the chest instead of the belly. Relaxation breathing exercises help you to reverse this habit, signaling to your autopilot that it is okay to stand down.

You'll find many breathing exercises online, and even a few apps to guide you. There are even "tactical breathing" apps for military, law enforcement, and others who are preparing for high-stress action to help keep their autopilots in a challenge, rather than threat, reaction.

Note: when doing these exercises, don't breathe so deeply that you become light-headed.

BELLY BREATHING

- Get comfortable. Lie on your back in bed or on the floor with pillows under your head and knees. Or you can sit in a chair with your shoulders, head, and neck supported against the back.
- Breathe in through your nose. Let your chest fill with air.
- Breathe out through your nose.
- Place one hand on your belly and the other on your chest.
- As you breathe in, feel your belly rise. As you breathe out, feel your belly lower. The hand on your belly should move more than the one on your chest.
- Take three more full, deep breaths. Breathe fully into your belly as it rises and falls with your breath.

4-7-8 BREATHING

You can do this sitting or lying down.

- To start, put one hand on your belly and the other on your chest as in belly breathing.
- Take a deep, slow breath from your belly, and silently count to four as you breathe in.
- Hold your breath and silently count from one to seven.
- Breathe out completely as you silently count from one to eight. Try to get all the air out of your lungs by the time you count to eight.
- Repeat three to seven times or until you feel calm.

Notice how you feel when you are done.

GROUNDING

When you are wound up, simply choosing to *notice* things around you can turn down the anxiety. This is called grounding because it helps you connect to the physical world. As with all relaxation techniques, an online search will yield plenty of guidance. Here's one that I've used and seen working for others. It's called "5-4-3-2-1."

- Name five things you can see in the room with you.
- Name four things you can feel right now.
- Name three things you can hear right now.
- Name two things you can smell right now (or, two things you like the smell of).
- Name one good thing about yourself.

Another approach to grounding is to "go shopping in your mind." Think about something that requires concentration: the order of books on your bookshelf or the order of songs in an album or playlist you like to listen to, for example. You don't have to do it for long—maybe thirty seconds or a minute, but the key is to be disciplined about it and do it each time that negative thought comes back—even if that means doing it many times an hour.

TAPPING

Later, when I describe therapies for trauma, I'll include a technique called eye movement desensitization and reprocessing, or EMDR. Despite the complicated name, EMDR is based on a simple principle: when our brain receives stimulation that alternates between its two sides, it relaxes. One of the important effects is to disconnect the emotions of a high-stress event from your memories of it, which allows you to recall the event without feeling as if you are back in it. Tapping isn't EMDR, but it is similar. There are many kinds of tapping; you can find entire books on it.

"Butterfly hug" tapping is easy. All you need to do is fold your arms over your chest, so that you can tap between your collarbone and shoulder. Let your mind go wherever it wants while you slowly tap yourself with each hand, alternating. Do this for thirty seconds. Most people find this relaxing. If you don't want what you're doing to be so obvious, you can do something similar by tapping your thighs alternately. It works a bit better if you cross your arms. You'll find more detailed descriptions online.

PROGRESSIVE MUSCLE RELAXATION (PMR)

PMR is based on tightening one group of muscles at a time, followed by relaxation. It helps activate renewal, relieve excess anxiety, help you sleep better, and more. You can do it while lying down or seated, but it will work best if you choose a place free of distractions. You may even fall asleep. Warming up with one of the deep breathing techniques can help prepare you.

- While inhaling, contract a muscle group (see below) for five to ten seconds, then exhale and suddenly release the tension.
- Give yourself ten to twenty seconds to relax, and then move on to the next muscle group.
- While releasing the tension, try to focus on the changes you feel when the muscle group relaxes. Imagery may be helpful, such as picturing stressful feelings flowing out of your body as you relax.
- Gradually work your way up the body contracting and relaxing muscle groups.
- Here are the muscle groups that you can focus on sequentially.

  - Forehead
  - Jaw
  - Neck and shoulders
  - Arms and hands

- Buttocks
- Legs
- Feet

An internet search will find more detailed instructions and audio recordings that will guide you through the process.

ROUTINE: MINDFULNESS

People who regularly practice mindful meditation rewire their brains, which modern imaging science captures.[21] Their prefrontal cortex (PFC), the area of the brain that puts *you* rather than your stress autopilot in charge, grows and increases its connections. Some of those connections give the PFC a greater ability to quiet the stress autopilot.[22] Mindful meditation brings you into the present, reducing anxiety from the past and worry about the future. You become less self-judgmental and more accepting of yourself as you are in the moment. Mindful meditation has been shown to activate renewal, decreasing "binary" (this-or-that) thinking and increasing your ability to see things from more than one viewpoint.[23]

Mindfulness is a key part of many mind-body practices, such as yoga, Pilates, tai chi, and martial arts. Although these build strength and flexibility, importantly, they also build your ability to notice what is going on with your body. Physiologists call this sense "interoception." It isn't entirely conscious and plays a vital role in your ability to regulate emotions. Mindfulness practices can shrink your brain's stress autopilot after it is enlarged by long periods of unrelieved stress.[24]

The scientific evidence that mind-body exercises help build resilience is extensive and growing. As Bessel van der Kolk has taught in depth, stressful and traumatic experiences are not just stored in our minds; they also change our bodies. Mind-body practices can help you feel safe inside yourself when your past keeps trying to draw you away from the present.

You can bring about some of these helpful changes in as little as eight weeks.[25] Most significantly, research shows that mindful meditation increases the kind of flexibility that builds resilience: the part of your brain that triggers stress responses becomes less sensitive and quiets down faster when you practice mindful meditation. At first, practicing it gives you more conscious control over your emotional reactions. Those who practice it long term appear to increase *acceptance*, rather than control, of their emotions.

This type of meditation also helps you become more deliberate about where you give your attention and how well you notice and process conflicting information.[26] Better control of attention is essential to well-being: your brain's "default mode" is to wander unhappily. Mindful meditation reduces default-mode activity, putting you more in charge of your life.[27]

During California's fire season, I sometimes volunteer at the Copernicus Lookout Tower for fire watch, which I eventually realized can be a relaxing exercise in mindfulness, even though it is related to the stress of firefighting. At 4,360 feet, Copernicus, adjacent to the Lick Observatory, is the highest point in the entire San Francisco Bay Area. On a clear day, we can see Monterey Bay to the west, Big Sur to the south, Yosemite's Half Dome to the east, and Mount Tamalpias in Marin County to the north. We need to stay in the present moment—mindfulness—because a fire can grow large very quickly. The faster we spot and report smoke, the greater chance of containing a fire while it is small. Building the habit of noticing when my attention has drifted is the essence of practicing mindfulness. Still, I always take time to appreciate the beauty of nature, especially as groups of raptors—mainly peregrine falcons and red-tailed hawks—seem to play in a valley next to the tower, swooping and diving, riding invisible air currents.

ROUTINE: SLEEP

Good sleep—long enough and deep enough—renews us from the stress of being awake, but it is far more than that. During sleep, we process emotions and memories, solidifying knowledge and enhancing creativity. You need sleep, like every other kind of stress and renewal, of the right quality and quantity, and at the right intervals. Insufficient sleep will cause you far more problems than not getting enough food or exercise.

Many of us are not getting enough good sleep, which dramatically affects quality of life and is likely to make most of the other guidance in this book ineffective. "Sleep Into Strength" is just as true as "Stress Into Strength." A 2004 study showed that 26 percent of American adults were not getting enough sleep.[28] In a larger survey, in 2014, only 65 percent reported a healthy sleep duration.[29] About half of the population reports difficulty falling or staying asleep. Less than 20 percent of those with insomnia are correctly diagnosed and treated; yet insomnia increases your odds of a mental disorder by a factor of four to eight.[30] The nations where average sleep duration has dropped the most—the United States, United Kingdom, Japan, and South Korea—have seen the greatest increase in sleep-related physical and mental problems.

Too little sleep results in altered hormone levels that make you crave the wrong foods and disrupt the hormonal signals that tell you when you are hungry (ghrelin) and full (leptin), contributing to weight gain[31] and making effective weight loss nearly impossible. Impulse control becomes more difficult, which contributes to behavioral problems and weight gain. Shortened sleep results in greater pain the following day, a 2008 research report showed.[32]

"Routinely sleeping less than six or seven hours a night demolishes your immune system, more than doubling your risk of cancer," warns Matthew Walker in his eye-opening, best-selling book, *Why We Sleep*. "Insufficient sleep is a key lifestyle factor determining whether or not you will develop Alzheimer's disease. Inadequate sleep—even moderate reductions for just one week—disrupts blood sugar level so profoundly that you would be classified as prediabetic. Short sleeping increases the likelihood of your coronary arteries becoming blocked and brittle, setting you on a path toward cardiovascular disease, stroke, and congestive heart failure." To your stress autopilot, failing to get good sleep (quantity, quality, or timing) signals danger or opportunity.

> Practice does not make perfect. It is practice, followed by a
> night of sleep, that leads to perfection.
>
> — MATTHEW WALKER

The quality of our sleep impacts our emotional and cognitive intelligence. Better sleep makes us sharper at recognizing social and emotional signals as we interact with others, while also improving our ability to regulate our own emotions. Matthew Walker suggests that our emotional intelligence, born of quality sleep, may be the most important factor that makes humans the dominant species on Earth, enabling us to create and sustain complex alliances and networks that accomplish far more than less-attuned individuals can. Meanwhile, our cognitive skills, refined during sleep, have given rise to myriad innovations and solutions.[33] Even if Walker is only partially correct, the societal impact of widespread sleep deprivation is enormous.

Poor sleep also leaves you more susceptible to posttraumatic stress injuries. Although we don't fully understand the mechanism, evidence shows that your brain processes trauma—letting go of memories you don't want or need—during deep, rapid-eye-movement (REM) sleep. If you don't get enough deep sleep to process trauma, traumatic memories are more likely to haunt you.

Much like missing other sources of renewal, when you aren't getting enough sleep, you may not even realize how sleep deprived you are. Test subjects in sleep-deprivation studies undergo "microsleeps," during which they are entirely unaware of their surroundings. (That is potentially deadly when driving—and unlike the slow reactions of a drunk driver, microsleeping drivers *do not react at all*.) Yet they consistently underestimate how impaired they are. Those who are chronically sleep deprived often begin to believe that their impairment is normal, rather than a deficit that could be fixed with quality sleep.[34]

Practice good sleep hygiene. Here are key tips:

- The National Sleep Foundation recommends the following duration of sleep (and only a miniscule percentage of people need less):
  - 14–17 hours for newborns
  - 12–15 hours for infants
  - 11–14 hours for toddlers
  - 10–13 hours for preschoolers
  - 9–11 hours for school-aged children
  - 8–10 hours for teenagers
  - 7–9 hours for young adults and adults
  - 7–8 hours of sleep for older adults
- Avoid stimulants (caffeine, nicotine), heavy meals, intense exercise, and emotion-charged entertainment close to bedtime.
- Naps are okay. A 2009 review of the literature on napping concluded that "napping is a practical solution to daytime sleepiness for shift workers and people with sleep disorders. But even for individuals who generally get the sleep they need on a nightly basis, napping may lead to considerable benefits in terms of mood, alertness, and cognitive performance."[35] Interestingly, one study found that only those who *habitually* nap find it restorative.[36] Nap or don't nap—there's no in between, apparently. Naps are most effective in the afternoon but not a good idea in the evening, when they can disrupt your ability to go to sleep at bedtime. Three p.m. is the cutoff recommended by experts. For most people, naps need to be at least ten minutes long, but no more than thirty minutes. But remember this—*napping does not replace the need for good sleep!*
- Manage light and darkness because they affect sleep, al-

tering hormone levels. Get into natural light during the day, for at least thirty minutes, and darken the room you sleep in.

- Avoid blue-tinted phone, computer, and other display devices before bedtime. If you use them, install software that automatically "warms" the screen hue as bedtime approaches.

- Establish a routine to signal your body that it is time to sleep—for example, a warm shower, aromatherapy, reading, or light stretching. Practice the breathing exercises or progressive muscle relaxation from this chapter to help get ready for sleep.

- The best room temperature for falling and staying asleep is sixty to sixty-seven degrees.

- Sticking to a regular sleep schedule is critical. A review of twenty-three years of data showed that more workers are injured, and the injuries are more serious, on the Monday after the United States switches to daylight saving time—a mere one-hour sleep loss.[37] Larger changes can take days of adjustment.[38] Matthew Walker, the author of *Why We Sleep,* suggests setting an alarm for when to go to bed. You cannot make up for lost sleep—and getting up too early robs you of one of the most important kinds of sleep.

- Don't watch TV, talk on the phone, or do business in bed. Make your bedroom a haven.

- Avoid substances that disrupt REM sleep, especially after trauma. These include alcohol and some antianxiety sleep medications, such as the benzodiazepines—alparazolam (Xanax), quazepam (Doral), triazolam (Halcion), estazolam (ProSom), temazepam (Restoril), flurazepam (Dalmane), and lorazepam (Ativan). Medication should be your last resort, but if you need it, be sure to ask your doctor for sleep aids that don't interfere with REM sleep. This is especially important in the aftermath of

psychological trauma—poor REM sleep raises your risk
of suffering posttraumatic stress. One of the most effective treatments for posttraumatic stress disorder (PTSD),
called eye movement desensitization and reprocessing
(EMDR), is theorized to reproduce the brain processing
that happens during REM sleep.[39]

■ Having trouble falling asleep because you are "tired and
wired"? Try watching a light comedy that you have already seen several times. Focusing on something familiar
helps—that's why you get so sleepy driving home then lie
awake wondering what changed!

■ Let go of pressure to sleep. Tell yourself, "I'm getting into
bed to rest" rather than insisting that you go right to sleep.
But don't lie in bed awake for long—get up and do something relaxing until you feel sleepy, then return to bed.
Feeling pressure to sleep will keep you awake.

■ Know how much sleep you need. Do you wake up rested?
If you think you might have a sleep disorder, start keeping
a sleep diary and tell your doctor. Untreated sleep apnea
has serious potential consequences. If you feel as though
you could fall back asleep at 10:00 or 11:00 a.m., or if you
cannot operate effectively without caffeine before noon,
you probably are not getting enough deep sleep, according to Matthew Walker. Check in with your doctor—a
sleep study is the only way to definitely figure out if you
are sleeping as well as you need to.

■ Experiment! Try these techniques until you discover what
works best for you.

■ A study in Australia showed that when people live closer
to green spaces, they were less likely to suffer short
sleep.[40] And a much larger U.S. study showed similar results.[41] In Japan, people suffering from sleep problems
who walked for two hours in a forest slept longer and
deeper than when they did not.[42]

- In two literature reviews, mindful meditation showed promise for helping with sleep difficulties.[43]
- Exercise and sleep can help or hinder each other. Moderate workouts will help you sleep better and avoid sleep disorders; better sleep helps you stay motivated to work out and avoid injury.[44] Although avoiding exercise before sleep formerly was part of the National Sleep Foundation's recommendations, research suggests that it doesn't interfere.[45]

You are likely to sleep better if you follow other guidance in this book, because anything that helps settle down your stress response removes obstacles to sleep.

ROUTINE: DIET

Turning stress into strength requires nourishment. For example, even with the ideal workout routine, your muscles cannot grow stronger unless you also get the right amounts of protein at the right intervals. Diet doesn't just affect your body; we are learning more every day about how it also affects your mind.

Just as an easy workout will not make you stronger, research shows that easy-to-digest foods leave you weaker. Highly processed foods are made from nutrients that have been extracted from their sources—sugars, oils, and so forth. They are easier to digest because your gut doesn't have to break them down; but easier-to-digest is not good for you. They lack fiber that stimulates your gut and feeds the organisms that live there, organisms vitally important to your physical and mental health.

When you eat, you're not just feeding yourself, you are also feeding the bacteria, fungi, and other microorganisms that live in your gut. Research is increasingly revealing that our health—physical and mental—depends on the types and variety in your "gut biome." Your gut and brain, connected by the vagus nerve and other body signaling systems, are much more dependent on each other than previously suspected. When you eat food that has not been highly processed, the "leftovers" that you can't digest become important food for your gut biome. Highly processed food has far fewer leftovers, which also means that more of the calories are going into you, making weight management more difficult.

An information superhighway connects your gut and brain—the vagus nerve, which, as you have already read, reflects your physical and mental health. Evidence is mounting that the state of your gut biome makes a tremendous impact on physical and mental health. To make matters more complicated, it is also clear that your mental state can impact your food choices, sometimes leading you to crave what is bad for you.

Although we know that gut health depends on having diverse organisms, due to the extreme complexity, nobody really knows what a healthy assortment is. We know that it will include more than a thousand types. Despite the popularity of probiotic supplements, they are no substitute for *foods* that are "probiotic" (fermented and other foods that contain a variety of helpful microorganisms) and "prebiotic" (those that feed your gut biome) because we have little specific knowledge of which varieties and proportions make up a healthy gut. (One of the downsides of taking strong antibiotics is that they reduce gut biome diversity.)

When stress dominates your life, rather than renewal, chronic inflammation results, which either worsens or improves with your diet. Inflammation is related to many health issues—diabetes, heart disease, Alzheimer's, and especially depression.[46] Sugars, other carbohydrates, and processed foods contribute to inflammation. Fish, especially fatty fish such as tuna, salmon, and anchovies, have Omega-3 acids, which help reduce inflammation.

Search the web for "anti-inflammatory diet" and you'll find quite a bit of relevant advice, but here are foods to avoid.

■ Highly processed foods. Watch out for snacks—they often have trans fats (bad for you) to increase their shelf life.

- Soft drinks. A twelve-ounce drink can contain the equivalent of twenty-five teaspoons of sugar.
- Anything labeled "low fat" or "low carb." These tend to stimulate your appetite and lead you to overeat.
- Fried foods.

You probably already know what a healthier diet looks like—a good balance of fruits, veggies, nuts, beans, seeds, and whole grains along with lean protein and healthy fats. One problem with shifting your diet is that it's so much *easier* to buy or prepare food that's bad for you. Try picking up a precooked rotisserie chicken, vegetables that you can steam in their bag, and other food that's healthy but simple to prepare. *Don't* add to your stressors by trying fancy new complicated recipes and such. Crash diets are a mistake because they amplify your body's stress reactions, so they backfire. There is increasing evidence that regularly eating fermented foods—some cheeses, yogurt, apple cider vinegar, red wine, sourdough bread, raw sauerkraut, kimchi—encourages a healthy gut biome and lower inflammation. And here's some really good news you may not realize—chocolate is a fermented food! Dark chocolate (which avoids the carbohydrates in other forms) contains both prebiotics and probiotics.

If you are working on muscle strength, you'll benefit from making sure you're getting protein before and after your workouts and in the morning. Watch out for dehydration—drink enough water to replace what you lose during exercise.

Eating mindfully is easy and rewarding. Slow down. Before taking a bite, look at your plate, smell, and begin to appreciate it. With each bite, take your time and savor the flavors. Set your fork down as you chew. Pause after swallowing, then pick up your fork and have another bite. You'll find that you'll eat less because you will more quickly notice you are full than when you wolf down less healthy fare.

Eating well is a tough challenge when your stress autopilot is stuck. The altered hormones conspire to make you crave carbohydrates, while confusing your senses of when you are hungry or full. In other words, an entire bag of potato chips (or your favorite high-carb junk food) looks really, really delicious when your autopilot is activated. "Stress eating" is all too real.

Cravings will diminish with time, but even if your resilience routines are hit-or-miss, you will be quieting down that noisy autopilot, which will give more energy to the part of your brain that gives you self-discipline and motivation. Keep in mind that these changes happen slowly, they create their own stress (especially if you overdo them), and backsliding is normal—start small and give yourself unlimited permission to fail and start over.

ROUTINE: CONNECTING WITH NATURE

According to a United Nations report updated in 2018, half of the world's population and 80 percent of U.S. residents live in urban areas, disconnected from nature unless they venture away from home.[47] Meanwhile, a 2013 comprehensive review of research into the effects of nature on our well-being[48] concluded, "The balance of evidence indicates conclusively that knowing and experiencing nature makes us generally happier, healthier people."[49] A study of almost twenty thousand English adults found that those who spent at least two hours a week in a natural environment were in better health than those who did not get as much exposure—even if the participants did not live in an area close to green spaces and regardless of the length of their visits. The researchers found this correlation to be present even for people suffering from long-term illnesses or disabilities, suggesting that it was not just that healthier people visit nature more often. Up to five hours a week, spending more time in nature corresponded to increasingly better health.[50]

Some doctors are now prescribing time in nature—"ecotherapy"—to improve mood. A frequently cited 2011 review of studies comparing indoor and outdoor exercise reported that "exercising in natural environments was associated with greater feelings of renewal and positive engagement, decreases in tension, confusion, anger, and depression, and increased energy."[51] The authors suggest that more rigorous research is needed.

Studies of natural environments specifically focused on stress have found that time spent in nature—and even living in proximity to green spaces—is associated with reduced stress response.

- Analysis showed that Danes living more than one kilometer from a green space reported poorer health and higher odds of feeling excess stress. Those who visited green spaces reported feeling stress less often.[52]
- Researchers in the Netherlands found similar patterns within a three-kilometer radius in two studies.[53]
- In Chicago, researchers found that parks in urban areas encourage social support, while vegetation in neighborhoods reduces it. In other words, green spaces are helpful but scattered greenery is not.[54]
- Analysis of incomes, health, and proximity to natural spaces in England showed that living closer to green areas reduced the inequalities in health that go with lower incomes.[55]
- A 2014 literature review observed that natural places are restorative, helping people relax their minds and bodies for reasons that include reduced complexity, intensity, and movement, compared with the overload that urban areas may induce.[56]
- Studies focused on economically disadvantaged urban communities have found lower cortisol levels correlate to access to green spaces.[57]
- Stanford University researchers sent test subjects on walks through a natural area near campus and others on an urban walk of the same distance. Those who spent time in nature were less anxious and likely to dwell on negative thoughts. Their "working memory"—the ability to keep information in mind as you analyze, learn, or

understand—also improved. The scientists followed this with brain scans, which showed a decrease in activity of the part of the brain responsible for the tendency to ruminate on negatives.[58] Other studies have shown that if there's running water nearby, a nature walk is even more beneficial.

A simple theory offers a possible explanation of why green spaces are relaxing: we don't have to maintain nature; it takes care of itself. Although in the modern world, green spaces need protection, no cleaning, dusting, vacuuming, painting, or other maintenance is necessary!

The "green exercise" movement is based on studies that show that exercising outdoors is better for both physical and mental health than indoors.[59] The "biophilia hypothesis" is that we have an innate need to connect with nature; disconnection is harmful.

Getting into nature can make exercise seem easier and improves motivation. One study observed, "When allowed to self-select walking speed, participants tend actually to walk faster outdoors, compared to indoors. Paradoxically, they report a lower rating of perceived exertion."[60] Monitoring has showed that runners exert less energy when running outdoors compared to a treadmill.[61] Nature may be helpful because it is distracting (the same has been found for music).[62]

Gardening also connects us with nature, with the same kind of benefits and more. We know that getting your hands dirty helps your immune system. Connecting with the natural world reminds us that it is normal for life to be messy, a constant interplay of birth, growth, death, and decay. Bringing nature to you is also effective—adding a plant to a room helps calm its occupants.

In Japan, "Forest bathing" (*shinrin-yoku*) became a medicinal practice as an antidote to urban life in the 1980s, but it has ancient roots in Asia. Kneipp therapy in Germany is a similar practice. Adrenaline and cortisol[63] levels drop, along with heart rates and (in some studies) blood pressure. It activates renewal,[64] in-

cluding boosting your immune system.[65] Researchers even analyze which forest components are most effective—the odors of
wood, the sound of running stream water, or the scenery.

Living near green space has been shown to be important for
mental health and is associated with longevity and decreased risk
of mental illness in Japan,[66] Scandinavia,[67] and the Netherlands.[68]

ROUTINE: TOUCH

When I was a paramedic in training at an emergency room in
Pittsburgh, I saw a note pinned to a staff bulletin board, reminding everyone to make sure that at some point in caring for patients, they should make physical contact, because studies
showed touch improves outcomes. Some joker had scribbled at
the bottom, "How can we perform miracles without laying on
hands?" There's a lot of truth in those words.

Touching and being touched, especially by people with whom
we are socially bonded, activates physical renewal. A research
review shows that it can reduce heart rate, blood pressure, and
cortisol levels while increasing the renewal hormone oxytocin;
moderate pressure massage decreased depression while enhancing the immune system.[69] Other reviews show that adding massage to medications for high blood pressure is more effective than
the drugs alone, although they concluded that further research is
needed to understand how it works.[70]

Infants, artificially stressed by their mother acting unavailable
to them, show a lower stress response and faster rebound if their
mother touches them.[71]

Hugging, huddling, and other kinds of touch have more than one
way of activating renewal. Through touch, we keep one another
warm, increase social bonding through increased renewal hormone
levels, and give each other physical care and consolation.[72]

Therapeutic touch helps cancer patients with pain, nausea,
anxiety, and fatigue, a recent research review showed.[73]

ROUTINE: MUSIC AND ART

Music and art, whether you are making them or enjoying them, can lower your stress response. Like almost everything else, if you feel a lot of pressure to perform, you may have more of a stress than renewal reaction, but studies show that when your *intention* is to relax, music and art can get the job done.[74] This is an area where research is limited, but what we see so far is encouraging. Even though I've put these in the physical resilience chapter, music and other forms of art often have social aspects and sometimes are spiritual, renewing a sense of beauty, awe, and wonder. In one small study, music was more effective than "stress reduction" strategies at self-calming.[75]

A study of sixty young women showed that listening to relaxing music[76] lowers the stress hormone cortisol faster than without it, compared with silence or listening to the sound of rippling water.[77] Another study challenged male and female undergraduates to prepare for an oral presentation. Those who first listened to relaxing music[78] showed fewer stress signs afterwards.[79]

Choir singing, with potential social benefits, has been studied more than individual singing. A long-term analysis of a group of young, healthy members of an amateur student choir showed improved mood and relaxation—especially *after* their first public performance of new music. The benefits were not associated with their social contacts within the choir, but the researchers suggested that if they studied singers who chose a choir specifically for the social contacts, those results might be different.[80]

Analysis of a small vocal jazz ensemble showed that stress hormone levels dropped and oxytocin increased as they entered a "flow state" of singing. Oxytocin rose significantly more when they improvised, suggesting that being more creative led to greater renewal and stronger social connections.[81]

Group drumming, often a component of social bonding rituals, has received some research attention, especially in the context of recovery and therapy. As nonverbal communication, drumming can create a sense of belonging to the group and increase social safety by supporting participation without judging or trying to "fix" others. It also appears to be yet another means of grounding.[82] Small studies have also observed improvement in well-being, reduction in aggression, and other benefits for at-risk adolescents[83] and people who care for them.[84]

Art is studied primarily as therapy rather than as a routine part of daily life. Research is quite limited, but a review concluded that, although more research is needed, art therapists' intuitive belief in its effectiveness is accurate. Art therapy has been applied to a wide range of ages in a variety of settings from schools to prisons, with statistically significant positive results.[85]

When our crisis intervention team responds to a school for the death of students or staff, we always suggest putting out paper and coloring supplies for people to create posters. The act of creating them seems to help survivors. We invite them to make one poster to keep at the school (which we counsel them to put in a place where it can be visited, but not constantly in view, giving people the choice about when to see it) and another to give to the family of the deceased. Giving people something to do in response to trauma is powerful. People clearly have a strong desire, if not a deep need, for "action steps" as our team leader, Janet Childs, calls them, that acknowledge loss. Witness the memorials that pop up at the site of violent deaths, with candles, cards, flowers, stuffed toys, and so forth.

social resilience routines: connecting with others

Look around is the *social* reminder. People surround you—family, friends, mentors, teammates. We are all in this together. We have a deep need for times and places when we can be real, be ourselves, warts and all. We also gain resilience from being others' trusted and reliable support. Social routines are those in which you give and receive acknowledgment, care, and support. They include teamwork, friendships, family, leaders and leadership, mentoring and being mentored, community and government.

Look around is the reminder to stay connected to the people (and companion animals) around you. Psychological research finds, over and over, year after year, that social support correlates to resilience more than anything else. We need other people and they need us. Everyone needs at least one or two close and supportive people. It's not just about receiving support—*giving* it is important to your well-being too. We need to be known, accepted, and loved for who we are, which are also the greatest gifts we can offer others. Social resilience routines strengthen us emotionally (empathy, compassion) and cognitively (safety, strategy). Social support isn't just about mental health. A review of studies with more than three hundred thousand participants showed that social relationships extend our lives as much as quitting smoking, while the lack of them adds more health risk than obesity and inactivity.[1]

Those who refresh others will be refreshed.

—PROVERBS 11:15

Adding social engagement is most important if you are a Challenger, Mediator, or Reformer. Connecting with people will build empathy, and help you become more transparent with others, reducing your sense of isolation. Social renewal will help you learn to stop treating other people as pawns in a game.

If you are a Helper, Achiever, or Individualist, you are engaged socially but often in an unhealthy way, putting others' opinions ahead of yourself as you seek to be needed, admired, or unique. In your social engagements, learning "what other people think of me is none of my business" is important so that you become more honest about yourself and *listen* rather than showing off. Practice not taking things personally by working on being an objective, accepting observer of yourself just as you are.

The relationship between social support and resilience makes sense—what could be better than knowing that family, friends, or an entire community accepts you as you are and has your back? What could be worse than feeling that nobody cares? In disaster planning, we know that networked communities are more resilient, because they are better at sharing resources, such as tools, skills, and priorities. We solve problems faster and more efficiently when we share the results of lots of independent trial and error. We learn from one another's struggles and triumphs.

Positive social interactions lead to happier, healthier, and longer lives.[2] Social support increases renewal hormone levels, lowers stress hormones, and reduces depression and anxiety.[3] Having compassion for others can help to quiet your stress response,[4] make you a better parent,[5] protect your children from excess stress,[6] and improve your sleep,[7] among the many benefits. Building compassion for self and others has also been shown to improve the resilience of therapists,[8] firefighters,[9] medical students,[10] nurses,[11] public service workers,[12] and many others. Even if you don't actually tap into social support, *just knowing someone cares* makes a big difference in your well-being.[13]

Social resilience routines are about our hearts: friendship, affection, communication, conversation, cooperation, competition, and teamwork. The rising trend of loneliness in our culture is deeply worrying because, without strong social support, people are far more likely to become addicted, commit crimes, kill themselves, and otherwise fail to cope well with life's ordinary stresses, much less trauma. We need social connection to help us cope with strong emotions, see ourselves more clearly, and accomplish things we cannot do on our own.[14]

Social support can be formal—faith meetings, 12-step programs, grief and loss groups, Toastmasters, Rotary, mentors, leaders, and others that nurture friendships, even if that is not their primary purpose. Support can also be informal, the care and companionship shared by friends, family, neighbors, hobbyists, sports or workout companions, coworkers, and animal companions. Remember that this isn't just about receiving; supporting others can lower your blood pressure, and you are more likely to receive support if you give it.[15]

Serving others may be the most effective way to activate renewal. Author Brené Brown says that she doesn't like her books appearing in the "self-help" section. If you want to help yourself, she says, help someone else.

The stress you'll feel from exercising your social "muscles" shows up as embarrassment, humiliation, judgment, and vulnerability. Those are natural when you choose to disclose things about yourself that you aren't proud of—or when others point them out. But remember, don't be in a big hurry. Take small steps out of your comfort zone; you can't grow strong overnight. Strength, in this context, means building confidence to *be yourself*.

Classes and books can help you to overcome fears and phobias, become more assertive, increase your self-esteem, and become a better conversationalist. Taking classes on a topic that interests you can be a way to find and make new friends.

COVID-19 has put limits on our ability to tap into in-person social support, but online social interaction was significant for many people before the pandemic. Social networking sites can offer support, but use caution. Stick to those that are reputable; be quick to leave a group that tolerates unhealthy behaviors—judgment, "fixing," breaking confidentiality, and breaking personal boundaries.

I do my best to follow a simple rule for filtering social media. If someone's postings trigger my self-righteous sense of outrage, I disconnect from them. I am quickest to hit the thirty-day "snooze" feature on Facebook when I feel as though I *must* get them to admit they are wrong. If I make a comment that leads to bickering, I delete it (which also deletes the replies and ends the argument). This seems to have had a positive side effect: I believe that I now see far fewer political posts, and not just because I've snoozed people. Facebook and other social media feed on *engagement*—your attention sells ads. If you don't engage with a topic, it will stop appearing in your feed.

exercising your social skills

I have described social stress as feeling isolated or lonely, embarrassed, betrayed, abandoned, criticized, guilty, or ashamed. We react to social stress with mental fight or flight by becoming defensive or distant, which disconnects us from people, and is sometimes the right thing to do. But when we get stuck in "defend and distance," genuine, strong connections to others become impossible. We become more isolated and lonelier, potent stress activators that can become a downward spiral.

Creating and maintaining social connections—the "weightlifting" of building social strength—means "getting real" with others, allowing safe, trusted companions to see you as you are and accepting feedback that you may deny or dislike, while doing the same for them. Like a tough physical workout, self-disclosure and feedback given and received in kindness and love often is painful and helpful at the same time.

Giving and receiving social support requires strong boundaries. Acceptance and compassion, the foundations of support, are impossible when we take advantage of, hurt, or take one another for granted. We need accountability, which is completely different from the addictive, relationship-destroying, self-righteous blaming and shaming that dominates social media. Healthy accountability requires separating who people *are* from what they *do*. We can accept and have compassion for people while creating consequences for their bad choices. When we don't do that for others, there isn't much hope of accepting or having compassion for ourselves, which are essential to our own resilience. In a twist on the saying "You can't give away what you don't have," the message here is, "You also can't have what you don't give away."

Fear of transparency and accountability is the big obstacle to receiving social support. Even though knowing ourselves and making deep connections with others helps us to grow stronger, we are often reluctant to reveal our struggles or who we really are. Embarrassment, guilt, and shame surface. (Like every other "negative" behavior, this reluctance surely serves a purpose—self-examination is a bad idea when it is time to seize an opportunity, rise to a challenge, or especially when a threat looms.)

Self-disclosure and accountability are especially difficult when you feel guilt or shame. In 12-step programs, the fourth step is "a searching and fearless moral inventory"—an accounting. Many, many 12-steppers come to a screeching halt at the prospect. Taking inventory is nothing more than accounting, yet it *feels* like judgment, especially to people mired in shame. But you cannot receive social support without becoming vulnerable. Your true self cannot receive love, care, or affection when it's hidden.

> As long as you keep secrets and suppress information, you are fundamentally at war with yourself. . . . The critical issue is allowing yourself to know what you know. That takes an enormous amount of courage.
>
> —BESSEL VAN DER KOLK

The same people terrified of doing a fourth step often look back after completing it and say that it really wasn't so bad. Having shared their "worst" with a trusted mentor, with much greater conviction they'll quote one of the program's mottoes—"You're only as sick as your secrets."

Perhaps inventory and disclosure look easier afterward because, by the time you have become willing to do them, you have let go of enough self-doubt, criticism, and judgment that you come to believe that *you are not what you do.* You're not. You are more than just what you do or have done.

> In a futile attempt to erase our past, we deprive the community of our healing gift. If we conceal our wounds out of fear and shame, our inner darkness can neither be illuminated nor become a light for others.
>
> —BRENNAN MANNING

My men's group can be one of the most uncomfortable places where I spend time, but that's because my brothers are willing and able (and sometimes, I fear, eager) to point out things about me that I can't or don't want to see. I have learned that the more I feel the urge to defend myself, the more likely their observations are correct! Although I acknowledge that my autopilot is reacting, I do my best to keep it from taking charge. By not going on the defensive, I'm much more open to asking myself, "Does this ring true?" Very often, thanks to the wisdom in our group, their feedback does.

Although criticism is often painful, thanks to our negative bias, it is more effective at motivating us than positive feedback. John Tierny, coauthor of a book on negative bias, *The Power of Bad: How the Negativity Effect Rules Us and How We Can Rule It,* suggests that a more effective version of the Golden Rule ("Do unto others as you want them to do unto you") would be, "Do not do unto others what you do not want done unto you."

In *The Gifts of Imperfection*, Brené Brown describes six types of "friends" who are not the kind of people you want to talk with about shame:

- The one who feels shame for you.
- The sympathetic one, who feels sorry for you.
- The one who is disappointed in you.
- The scold.
- The one who focuses on fixing and making you feel better.
- The one-upper, who tells an even "better" story.

These are not only warnings about who not to confide in, but they also represent the kind of person you must try not to be when others come to you with their stories of guilt and shame. And when you fail and realize you are being this kind of person, find someone who truly is compassionate to talk to about it. Shame cannot survive compassionate connections.

Language similar to the Golden Rule is a feature of Christianity, Islam, Taoism, Sikhism, Confucianism, and Jainism. Other religions offer the "negative" version—Judaism, Hinduism, Buddhism, Baha'i, and Zoroastrianism.

Trust and reliance on others are risky—that's why they activate the stress autopilot. American individualism can be an obstacle to exchanging social support, despite the fact that, in general, people see themselves more positively when they view themselves as interdependent, rather than independent.[16]

"If we help people who belong to our group, we're also helping ourselves, as we're making the group better off," writes Adam

Grant in *Give and Take: Why Helping Others Drives Our Success.* "People are just a bit more enthusiastic, friendly, and open-minded when they meet someone who reminds them of themselves." Likewise, the more others resemble us, the more of their pain we feel (vicarious stress and trauma).

We are pulled in two directions—we want to fit in and belong, making significant connections with others, but we also seek to be unique. Work too hard to belong (the Helper personality type) and you can lose your uniqueness; focus too much on uniqueness (the Romantic personality type) and you can lose your sense of belonging.

Giving and receiving social support works best when belonging and uniqueness are balanced. Whether we feel like we are giving more than we are receiving or vice versa, our well-being suffers, physically and mentally. In other words, at those times when you are getting a lot of support, it may become more important to give support to others.[17]

To avoid taking on too much social stress, all of us need freedom to choose *when* to talk about our struggles and *whom* to talk to. Trust does not happen overnight. When you find a sympathetic ear, you may have a strong urge to confess, to spill your guts with a person or group you are just getting to know. That's rarely a good idea. That's trying to "lift too much weight" than you're ready for. You may leave the group thinking "What did I just do?" and never go back. Get to know people first. Taking your time will also reduce the possibility that others will violate your trust. Honestly sharing your story can be overwhelming. Give yourself and others plenty of room and patience.

Take your time before speaking. Are you in the habit of thinking about what you want to say while another person is talking? When you notice you are in a rush to speak, come back to the present and really *listen.* Slow down, take a moment to listen to your intuition before adding your two cents. If you notice that you speak the moment the other finishes (or worse, sooner, interrupting!), that's much more likely to be your stress autopilot *reacting* rather than your true self *responding.*

Are your social interactions mostly complaints, gossip, insults, or being disagreeable? Aim for "daring and delightful," in the words of Sakyong Mipham, author of *The Lost Art of Conversation*. Bring "fierce affection" and "genuine curiosity," suggests Susan Scott, author of *Fierce Conversations*.

Curiosity is powerful, but it needs to be the right kind to be helpful. Instead of wondering "What's wrong with you?" invite a story: "What happened to you?"

I have no special talents. I am only passionately curious.

—ALBERT EINSTEIN

Psychologist Jordan Litman came up with a powerful distinction about curiosity: it can be driven by *interest* or by feeling *deprived*. The modern acronym FOMO (Fear of Missing Out) is an example of deprivation curiosity. Notice that the first word is fear, a stress activator. Deprivation curiosity conflicts with giving social support because it is about *getting* what you want; interest curiosity is *giving* of yourself. Our crisis intervention team sees this in volunteers. Some show up driven by deprivation curiosity—they want to know what it is like to do the job of firefighter, police officer, or other public safety worker. They end up seeking information about *what happened,* rather than making a more genuine, caring connection by inviting others to share how they experienced a critical incident—what they were thinking, how they reacted. "Deprivation feels closed and interest feels open," psychologist Jud Brewer observes.[18] He describes deprivation curiosity as "scratching an itch" and interest curiosity as "joyful exploration."

A well-run crisis intervention, driven by compassion for others rather than desire to join the drama, helps to quiet the participants' sticky stress reactions, allowing them to return to their usual level of functioning faster. It is also good for those who lead the intervention—recall that *caring creates resilience.* "With interest, the process of being curious feels good. It's its own reward,"

Brewer observes. I should note that in public safety, after major incidents, reviewing what happened is also important and supportive. We hold operational debriefings, also called hot washes, to review what went well and what we'd like to do better next time. The idea is to learn from experience, which research shows also helps quiet stress reactions. But everyone in these debriefings already knows what it's like to do the job. They aren't "scratching an itch."

> Unless someone like you cares a whole awful lot, nothing is going to get better. It's not.
>
> —DR. SEUSS, *The Lorax*

Giving social support is mostly about being present and listening, without judgment. To avoid losing your curiosity, avoid concluding that you have become an expert at it, which can lead you to stop listening. "I'm not an expert, I'm just experienced," I tell people about my years of crisis intervention.

Learning to stay present in conversations means developing a greater respect for your own words as well as others. The stress of honestly sharing your weaknesses or struggles can trigger your tend-and-befriend instinct, deepening your relationships. With practice, you will become better at this over time. Here are some ways to avoid getting social support wrong.

■ Guilt and shame are obstacles, not solutions. Crossing from support into shaming, rejection, or intimidation sets off a threat reaction, the social equivalent of dropping way too much weight on your friend who is doing a bench press. That will divide rather than bond you. It's *never* your job to make others feel guilty or ashamed. This is a big, ugly myth, easy to fall into. Although guilt and shame are natural feelings, useful reminders that we're doing something wrong, they are terrible motivators in the long run. They are autopilot activators, raising anxiety, anger, and worry, while robbing us of focus and willpower, encouraging distractions and procrastination. *Relief* from guilt and shame, in the form of unconditional acceptance, unlocks the door to self-improvement. It is the difference between "You did a bad thing" and "You are a bad person." Good people do bad things sometimes. You are not what you do. Confession to trustworthy companions often helps to release guilt and shame.

■ Invite. Don't pressure. Never push, poke, or prod others into talking about painful or difficult topics, especially if you suspect they feel guilty or ashamed. Remember that *having control* calms the stress autopilot. Pressuring others takes away control and will usually make them more defensive, distant, and distrustful. Invitations are okay; pressure is not. Recognize that trust can be deeply difficult after trauma. Pressure is likely to push them toward shame's accomplices, silence and secrecy. Patience and compassion, not coercion and pressure, make social support work its magic. *Invite* others to talk about their struggles; never demand. Walk beside them; don't imagine you can take them where you think they should go (an arrogant notion). The only way to help another person talk about their most difficult subjects is to be a safe, trustworthy person to talk to—confidential, accepting, nonjudgmental. At the beginning of every crisis intervention, I try to remember to say, "I'm not here to fix this or make it better." That's as much a reminder to myself (because I have a strong dose of the Helper personality) as information for those I'm talking with.

We resent being talked to. We'd rather be talked with.[19]

—SUSAN SCOTT

▪ Know the difference between compassion, empathy, and sympathy. Compassion is more important than empathy. There is no question that supportive people have empathy—the ability to feel what another person is feeling. We are wired to mirror one another's emotions, although the degree varies. Compassion is the urge to give companionship, comfort, or help when we see someone struggling or suffering. Empathy without compassion can lead us to look away and avoid feeling others' pain. Empathy connects you to others—it says, "I know that feeling too." Empathy doesn't require understanding. Even though you may not understand what another is going through, you can acknowledge the feeling. "That must be awful," shows empathy. It says "Me too" to the feeling, even if you haven't had the same experience.

▪ In Uganda, when there's a death, rather than saying "I'm sorry" or another sympathetic, distancing cliché, people say, "I stand beside you." Empathy means you are accompanying, without falling into pity, judgment, fixing, or other behaviors that distance you from others' pain. If that makes empathy sound painful, it is.

▪ Sympathy isn't helpful. It isn't quite as distancing as pity, but sympathy fails to connect us. It says, "Oh, you poor thing"—concern that something bad happened, but it doesn't say, "Me too."

▪ Don't try to fix other people or allow them to try and fix you. Watch out for prescriptive words and phrases like *should, ought to,* and *need to.* Trying to change another person's behavior is a put-down: it implies that they are not acceptable as they are. Even urging another to "make good choices" when fear, guilt, or shame have a hold on them (which you may not be able to see) is worse than useless. This doesn't mean people aren't responsible for bad behavior. Boundaries and consequences are fine when you are not trying to change them. Ask yourself, "What's my intent?"

- Resist the temptation to solve others' problems. This is especially difficult for men and particularly for those whose work focuses on problem-solving. Watch Jason Headley's wonderfully true and hilarious two-minute video *It's Not About the Nail,* which you can find on You-Tube.
- Social support has to be confidential. Nothing destroys trust faster than gossip.
- Beware of groups that proclaim, "Everyone is welcome," if membership depends on following their definition of good behavior. Such groups are inviting you to fit in rather than to belong. Eventually, false belonging based on "goodness" will reveal disconnection.

> Those who have a strong sense of love and belonging have the courage to be imperfect.
>
> **—BRENÉ BROWN**

Activating your renewal reactions raises oxytocin, the social bonding hormone, which has some surprising effects. Researchers found that giving it to people in relationships seemed to help them forget past romantic partners.[20] It appears that oxytocin bonds partners partly by helping them to forget the competition! The same study found if oxytocin improved recall of conflicts with their current romantic partner, the relationship was more likely to end. In other words, your response to extra oxytocin may reveal the strength of your current relationship.

ROUTINE: NOTICING AND ACKNOWLEDGING

Getting real, being transparent with trusted companions, means being vulnerable. Unfortunately, we tend to see vulnerability as courage in other people but weakness in ourselves. Remember that it is courage; it contributes to personal growth, even after trauma.[21] Treat yourself with as much compassion as you would give a friend or loved one.

> When a man or woman is truly honest, it is virtually impossible to insult them personally.
>
> —**BRENNAN MANNING**

Telling your story, putting feelings into words, helps you manage negative emotions.[22] It makes your stress autopilot less reactive while building up the part of your brain responsible for positive emotions. You can even "rewrite" your story as a more objective viewer of yourself, a powerful way to transform stress into strength.

Trusted friends can help you to become a fearless, nonjudgmental observer of yourself, better able to acknowledge and let go of the thoughts and reactions that come to you automatically under stress. The more you practice this, the better you will become at remaining calm and thoughtful, staying in challenge mode rather than threat mode. Psychologists call this "self-distancing."[23] It helps stop your stress autopilot from drowning out your rational thoughts. Over time, you'll find that you acquire a few more seconds of *thinking* before reacting.

Instead of beating yourself up, when your self-observation tempts you to judge, try curiosity and compassion. Why did a part of you feel something else was more important? Remember the distinction between interest and deprivation curiosity. Apply it to yourself too. Observe your own reactions with compassion, not as a problem to solve. Don't ask yourself, "What's wrong with me?" but curiously explore "What happened to me?" What experiences trained your stress autopilot?

Of course, you won't really be a *fearless* observer of yourself. Nobody is. Fear serves a purpose. Every "hero" I have met after high-stress and traumatic incidents, as well as those who have courageously revealed weakness or failure in my presence, was fearful at the time. They went ahead and did what needed to be done for others or themselves *despite* their reluctance. They had learned to ignore the internal voice warning, "Don't do that!" Nothing courageous ever happens without vulnerability.

Whatever you notice about yourself, no matter how pleased, proud, guilty, or ashamed you might feel, those traits are not as important as *getting in the habit of noticing.* "Taking notice" is the real meaning of the word *accountability,* which we often confuse with punishment and other consequences.

One of my mentors used to tell me (befuddling my perfection-ism), "Eighty percent is perfect." Judging what you notice isn't the point of self-observation; you are just *getting in the habit of notic-ing,* as you read about in focused-attention meditation.

Writing can be powerful self-observation. Consider keeping a journal, especially at times when you expect stress to be extra high. Sometimes it helps to write letters to people who wronged you or those you feel you wronged or let down. Try freeing your-self by writing only for yourself. I've found that after writing such letters, sending them often seemed unimportant.

My younger sister, Lesley, died quite suddenly in January 2010. Soon after, I found myself at a dinner getting acquainted with Jesse Mendoza, executive director of Jordan International Aid, which was sending medical teams to Haiti after the devastating earthquake, which happened eight days after Lesley died. She had lived in the Caribbean for about ten years, teaching English at the high school in Charlotte Amalie, St. Thomas.

"I think I need to go with you to Haiti," I told Jesse. Going would be impractical, but my intuition was strong; this would honor Lesley.

Everything came together: I found funding, got my immuniza-tions, and prepared to head out. The head of our Critical Incident Stress Management Team, my friend Janet Childs, who never tells anybody what they should do, almost ordered me to take a journal and write in it every day. I'd signed up to be the team's chaplain along with my medical duties, and she was concerned.

A couple of days before we left for Haiti, I realized how I would use the journal. Each entry begins, "Dear Lesley." That little book became a powerful and effective way to do the thing that I absolutely did not want to do, yet needed to: say goodbye.

ROUTINE: HOLD ON OR LET GO

At the end of each day on a disaster response like the Haiti mission, I like to gather the team for a short debriefing. I invite them to share their thoughts and reactions during the day's mission.[24] In a place like Haiti after the devastating earthquake, with overwhelming needs and few resources, emotions run high. We close the session with two questions: "What do you want to hold onto?" "What do you want to let go of?"

Noticing and acknowledging your reactions can free you to choose to hold on to or let go of them. Hold on to whatever gives you energy, builds your spirit, motivates you, reminds to you to be grateful and generous. Let go of whatever takes energy, holds you back, or weighs you down.

Letting go can sometimes be difficult, but *making the decision* is simple. There's an old saying about two frogs sitting on a log. One decides to jump off. Now how many frogs are on the log? The correct answer is two.

Sometimes all it takes to lighten your load is to become aware of it. If your stress "backpack" slowly and steadily becomes heavier, it's easy for the creeping increase in weight to feel normal. Instead of noticing the excess weight, you might just feel tired or irritable or have other symptoms of a stuck stress reaction.

"What do you want to hold onto?" "What do you want to let go of?" Those two questions help you take a mental step back, to notice and acknowledge your reactions. Only then can you decide to hold on to whatever gives you energy or to let go of whatever uses it up. You can become better at this by picturing yourself as if through a camera in the corner of the room. By imagining another person's point of view, you will be able to notice more of your own automatic reactions and you will be less tempted to judge them.

Noticing brings its own stress. You may recall painful memories, especially if layers of stress or trauma weigh you down. You may feel overwhelmed. You might get choked up or cry. In this disconnected world, many of us are carrying a lot of stress. It's tempting not to pay attention, in hopes of avoiding stress. But the only way we let go of difficult feelings is by *acknowledging, accepting, and experiencing them.* Although we vary in our need for social support, there is little or no substitute for supportive friends, mentors, or others to help this happen.

ROUTINE: WHO IS ON YOUR BOARD OF DIRECTORS?

Psychologist Frank Ochberg developed the idea that each of us has an internal "board of directors"—people from our past who continue to influence our thoughts, feelings, and decisions. Parents and guardians usually have the strongest voices, "telling" us decades later that we're good or bad. You didn't get to choose your family or others who are on your internal board of directors, but you can decide who you want today.

Consider building professional and personal boards of supportive people with diverse points of view. Don't include your spouse or significant other—they're in their own category. For professional support, choose two peers from the same level of your own occupation, along with at least one person from outside. For your personal board, a similar strategy would be to include two people whose opinions are mostly aligned with yours but at least one who shares your core values but sees the world differently.

Once you have picked candidates, decide what your expectations are—how and when you'll meet, how often, where, and so forth. Approach them individually, to see if they are willing to become part of your support network and can meet your expectations.

Expect some rejection. That will happen, but take the risk of asking anyway.

I have had this kind of support from several friends for decades and I cannot imagine life without them. When one had a fiftieth birthday party, I realized that we have eaten more than a thousand breakfasts together! One of my weekly meetings is with a friend whom I began mentoring years ago. I am no longer his mentor because we deliberately chose to become mutual supporters instead. As I began to share much more about my own struggles, we discovered that we have uncannily similar family backgrounds.

ROUTINE: LEARNING

We are individuals, but we are also social creatures. We influence others and they influence us. Although we can learn, feel, and do a great deal on our own, much of our knowledge, reactions, and accomplishments draw deeply from the people around us. Others don't merely impart knowledge; they give us motivation, direction, reassurance, criticism, rewards, punishment, and more. Our mental and emotional world is a product of genetics, experiences, and interactions.

Appropriate stress is essential to learning. No one ever became educated or wise because another person made it easy. A great leader, whether a yoga teacher or Marine Corps drill sergeant, knows how much stress to put on students, how hard to push them out of their comfort zone. Too little and they won't reach their potential. Too much and they may break or give up.

On the way to work for a summer at Yellowstone National Park, I stopped at Eldorado Canyon, near Boulder, Colorado, in late May, eager to do some rock climbing. Traveling alone, I had to choose climbing partners I didn't know much about. One of my choices almost killed me. The other one boosted my confidence.

My gut was uneasy about the first partner, but nobody else was around. My opinion of him dropped when he refused to allow another group to start the climb adjacent to ours, even though they were ready before us. The first "pitch," about a hundred feet, went well. I secured myself and belayed him as he headed up the second. The wind started rising and we began to hear thunder in the distance. The group he'd been rude to quickly exited their climb, but they stayed at the base to make sure we would be okay. Meanwhile, I was having trouble communicating with my partner, who had worked his way sideways and back, putting a lot of friction on his rope. I kept asking if he was in a secure spot, so that I could rappel off.

We were wearing shorts and T-shirts; when the rain began, I knew that hypothermia would result rapidly. I wanted to get off that rock. At last, my partner said he was clipped into a secure anchor.

The other group offered to let me use one of their ropes so that I wouldn't have to leave mine in place after I rappelled, so I hauled it up. I was shivering in the cold rain and wind. Thank goodness I had the presence of mind to triple-check my gear before starting the rappel. We always double-check, but a part of my mind, knowing I probably wasn't thinking very clearly, led me to look a third time. I saw that instead of clipping into my safety harness, I had clipped into my bandoleer—a piece of nylon webbing for holding equipment that hung loosely over my shoulder. If I'd rappelled that way, I'd probably have fallen right out of it, to my death.

I decided to pay more attention to my intuition when I chose my next partner. He was a British guy who had stories of climbing mountains all over the world. I was comfortable with him, and we decided to climb a route called Wind Ridge, which my new partner assured me wasn't difficult. I had told him that I didn't like "roofs," the climbing term for overhangs, so I was surprised when I got near the top to see the rope going over a difficult-looking roof.

"Come on up," he shouted. "There's big buckets on top!" ("Buckets" is climber jargon for big handholds.) Annoyed with him, I dragged myself up and over the roof and was surprised and a bit proud that I did it.

Back on the ground, I asked some climbers if Wind Ridge was really rated as a difficult beginner's climb—it seemed a lot harder than that. Yes, everyone told me, it is. Later, looking at a guidebook, I realized he'd tricked me. Wind Ridge is not a difficult climb, but it goes *around* the roof. We'd climbed Wind Ridge Direct, which is significantly harder.

That's a good teacher. I can forgive him for misleading me because he helped me discover that I could climb something I'd never have attempted on my own.

Good coaches, mentors, and teachers respect, motivate, and encourage you but aren't afraid to confront and offer constructive criticism. They also know that handholding eventually backfires and sometimes it is best to leave you on your own to figure things out. *What* you learn from others can make you more resilient by transferring skills that will help you bounce back. *Who* you know can make you resilient by giving you a network of people and their resources to tap into when disaster strikes. For example, if you have a strong social support network and your house burns down, you're far more likely to find a temporary place to stay than would someone without strong connections. If you don't have the right wrench, a friend or trusted neighbor probably does. Sometimes resilience is that simple. We are stronger together.

This principle also applies to communities. Resilient Communities Are Connected Communities is the name of a program of the CDC Foundation, created by the U.S. Congress to support the Centers for Disease Control. The Red Cross, FEMA, and other disaster relief organizations have similar mottoes and slogans. Individuals, neighborhoods, cities, and nations are more resilient when they know whom they can turn to in times of trouble. In the fire service, we call this "mutual aid," and we'd be in big trouble without it, especially during disasters like California's wildfires.

ROUTINE: SEEING INTO YOUR BLIND SPOTS

We need others' eyes to see into our blind spots. You might not see yourself as irritable, for example, but everyone else does. We all know people who think they are funny, but they're not. Bullies sometimes see themselves as "decisive." There is a Silicon Valley joke that leaders who think they are confident often are merely arrogant. We need others to be a mirror, even though seeing things we don't like about ourselves is usually uncomfortable.

As an analyst, it was my job to doubt and challenge Apple co-founder Steve Jobs. He seemed like a person who wouldn't care what anyone else thinks about his ideas. "Everybody gets a vote, but only Steve's counts." Yet he not only tolerated but seemed to encourage my criticism, regularly giving me the privilege of asking the first and last questions at briefings. One stands out.

I had challenged Steve's prediction of demand for a new computer. Steve sarcastically replied with, "Well, maybe after the briefing, you can come teach me about marketing." That got a big laugh. I countered, "Okay, but I'll have to charge you for that," which got an even bigger laugh. If Steve truly had a big, fragile ego, one-upping him probably would have raised an obstacle between us. But the opposite happened. He invited me to a tour of a new, ultramodern manufacturing facility, and I was astonished to find one of his family members accompanying us. Notoriously private, Steve always kept business and family separate. Later, as I read others' stories like mine in his biography, I finally realized that Steve didn't just tolerate criticism, he *wanted* to hear it. Even though he could bristle in reaction, at the end of the day, he knew the value of seeing his work through others' eyes.

> Your time is limited, so don't waste it living someone else's life. Don't be trapped by dogma—which is living with the results of others' thinking. Don't let the noise of others' opinions drown out your own inner voice.
>
> **—STEVE JOBS**

Ironically, many entrepreneurs seek to imitate Steve, who preached "be yourself." His vulnerability truly is worth imitating. Steve even eventually shrugged off an enormously painful rejection—getting kicked out of Apple—by choosing not to take it personally, much to the surprise of those around him.[25]

Our blindness isn't limited to our flaws and failures. We sometimes need our eyes opened to our gifts and strengths. You might not be aware that you are usually compassionate, but the people around you can see it. Ideally, your friends, teachers, and mentors help you see more positives than negatives about yourself, to counter your built-in negative bias. Those who can see you not just as you are but also as who you *could be* are a great blessing.

Here's a blind spot joke. A job interviewer asks about the interviewee's people skills. "How are my people skills? What a stupid question! People skills are my greatest strength—everybody knows that, you idiot!"

As I described in the context of building flexibility, we are most often blind to our gifts becoming liabilities when we rely too much on them. Excess empathy leads to self-neglect. Analysis becomes failure to act. Passion turns into arrogance, manipulation, and dominance. Yet we have trouble seeing what we are really doing.

I've sat with more than one workaholic who swears devotion to family. These people say they would never, ever abandon their family. Yet as we talk, I realize that's exactly what they've allowed, by working overtime or multiple jobs. They're still providing *things*—the paychecks can become big when you work that much. But they are no longer present or well connected to the family they say they care about.

When I see this pattern, I gently but firmly reflect it. I've been on the other end of that kind of confrontation. It's uncomfortable, but as I said earlier, I've learned that the more distress I feel, the more likely the other's observation is correct!

ROUTINE: SILENCING YOUR INNER CRITIC

Learning to see yourself *without judgment* is difficult but essential. You may have an overdeveloped critical inner voice, telling you that nothing is good enough, that *you* are not enough. Like so many other psychological struggles, this habit surely served a legitimate purpose in your early life. In adulthood, it is an obstacle, an anchor of guilt and shame. Supportive friendships can trigger that critic with their feedback, but they also can help you learn to set it aside so it is no longer in charge.

Getting out of the habit of criticizing others can help silence the habit of criticizing yourself. Friends can gently point out when you are should-ing on yourself. Remember that support doesn't mean giving advice or should-ing on other people. Codependents Anonymous offers a simple two-word summary of its program: "Don't Criticize."

> Real freedom is freedom from the opinions of others. Above all, freedom from your opinions about yourself.
>
> **—BRENNAN MANNING**

Here is an antidote to excess anxiety triggered by criticism: tell yourself, "What other people think of me is none of my business." That may sound ridiculous, but here are some reasons it is true.

- You are not a mind reader (even though you sometimes act as if you are). Guesses about what other people think of you are often wrong, driven by your negative bias.
- You have no control of what other people think. Trying to control the uncontrollable is a recipe for frustration, anger, and resentments.
- If others' opinions of you are important, you will take what they say personally, rather than recognizing that

their criticism comes from their own negative bias and life experiences. A great deal of what people have to say about you is really about them, but that is hard to see until you notice yourself doing it.

■ Worrying about what others think of you is a distraction.
■ People pleasing is a trap.

Here's a parable about worrying about what others think:

Two monks, who have taken a vow to have no contact with women, come to a river where a woman asks for help crossing. To the younger monk's astonishment, the older one carries her across. They continue their journey for a while. The younger monk finally can't hold his tongue and says, "We aren't supposed to have anything to do with women—why did you carry her across the river?" The older monk replies, "I set her down on the other side of the river. Why are you still carrying her?"

We instinctively do care what other people think of us. We have the power, however, to decide *which* people's opinions matter. That's what the "board of directors" is about—choosing whose opinions matter to you. Select people who have shown up for life—those who have fallen, failed, and known heartbreak, rather than those offering empty criticism "from the cheap seats," as Brené Brown says.

Find people who care *because* of your flaws, not despite them. That is true acceptance. Strive for courage to accept the least acceptable people around you, and you will surely know that you, yourself, are acceptable exactly as you are.

routines for renewal from social stress

"Knowing there are other people struggling with the same things I am makes all the difference," said a friend who had begun attending Al-Anon meetings. It's that simple sometimes. The power of another's simple acknowledgment—as simple as, "Wow, that sucks"—still surprises me, decades after I began to learn to stop trying to fix the unfixable and to be present to others.

One morning, after I'd spent the night providing peer support following a mass shooting, I began to talk to my wife about the toughest story we'd heard: a father trying to protect his daughter; she was killed even as he held her. While the story remained in my head, it was powerful but not overwhelming. But the moment I tried to speak, I choked up and could not talk at all. A few deep, autopilot-calming breaths later, I was able to talk and release a lot of the stress I was holding onto. That was a strong reminder that we can so easily kid ourselves about how we are doing—and how incredibly important it is to talk with people we trust.

You cannot receive social support without becoming vulnerable. Your true self cannot receive love, care, or affection when hidden.

"Vulnerability is not weakness; it's our greatest measure of courage," writes Brené Brown, whose books on courage, vulnerability, shame, and compassion are the stuff of social support. Vulnerability, Brown says, is having the courage to show up when you can't control the outcome.

> There is something within us that responds deeply to people who level with us.
>
> —SUSAN SCOTT

When trusting and trustworthy people "get real" with one another, everyone's good wolf is fed. Short of miracles, I'm not sure that anything is more powerful than to see and be seen by others exactly as we are, without judgment. In my experience, this is also the context in which seemingly miraculous healing and restoration happen.

We are all tempted, when feeling strong emotions welling up, to change the subject. It's okay if you do . . . sometimes. But you will still be carrying those feelings. I often remind myself and others that there is only one way to get rid of bad feelings: *name them and have them. We* don't *get over* or *move on*; our only choices are avoidance (unhealthy in the long run) or *to go through* the tough stuff, to learn to live with it.

ROUTINE: LOVING-KINDNESS AND COMPASSION MEDITATIONS

Not all kinds of meditation are the same. In contrast to the calming power of mindful meditation, loving-kindness and compassion meditations take energy.[26] Studies of these types of meditations show benefits for interpersonal conflict, the strain of long-term caregiving, social anxiety, marital conflict, and anger.[27] A pilot trial showed it has promise for reducing pain, anger, and psychological distress in patients with persistent lower back pain.[28]

Loving-kindness and compassion meditation increase social connectedness, building trust and cooperation while increasing well-being.[29] You may find it uncomfortable and awkward at first. It uses energy and requires time to begin to make a noticeable difference, but you will find that you will let yourself off the hook more often.

1. Choose some quiet time. Even a few minutes will work. Sit or lie down, whatever is comfortable for you. Close your eyes, relax your body, and notice your breathing. You may take a few deep breaths.
2. Imagine experiencing complete physical and emotional wellness and inner peace. If you wish, think of a person who loved or loves you unconditionally, perhaps when you were a child. You may also imagine feeling perfect love for yourself, thanking yourself for all that you are. Focus on the feeling of inner peace. Imagine that you are breathing out tension and breathing in feelings of love.
3. Choose or make up three or four positive, reassuring phrases to say to yourself. Imagine the best phrases that will open your heart of kindness. Here are some examples:

- May I be free from danger; may I know safety.
- May I be free of danger; may I be peaceful.
- May I have mental happiness.
- May I have physical happiness.
- May I have ease of well-being.
- May I be happy.
- May I be healthy, peaceful, and strong.
- May I give and receive appreciation today.
- May I accept my pain, without thinking it makes me bad or wrong.
- May I accept my anger, fear, and sadness, knowing that my vast heart is not limited by them.
- May I remember my consciousness is much vaster than this body.
- May all those who have helped me be safe, be happy, be peaceful.
- May all beings everywhere be safe, be happy, be peaceful.
- May my love for myself and others flow boundlessly.
- May the power of loving-kindness sustain me.
- May I be peaceful and happy, at ease in body and mind.
- May I be free from anger, fear, and worry.
- May I live and die in ease.

4. Allow yourself to feel warmth and self-compassion for a few moments. If your attention drifts, gently redirect it back to the feelings of loving-kindness.
5. After you have practiced this long enough that the awkwardness is gone (which can take a few weeks) you may choose to begin to include someone you love or care about. Begin with someone who you are close to: a spouse, child, parent, or best friend. Feel your gratitude and love for them. Stay with that feeling. You may want to repeat your positive phrases toward them:

- May you be free from danger; may you know safety.
- May you be free of danger; may you be peaceful.
- May you have mental happiness.
- May you have physical happiness.
- And so forth.

6. Once you've held these people in your thoughts, bring other important people from your life into your awareness, one by one, and picture them with wellness and inner peace. Then you may include other friends, family members, neighbors, and acquaintances. You may even want to include groups of people from around the world. Focus on feelings of connection and compassion.

7. Include difficult people, those with whom you are in conflict, seeking to forgive for greater peace.

8. When you feel your meditation is complete, open your eyes. Remember that during each day, you can revisit the state of compassion you generated. Return by shifting your focus and taking a few deep breaths.

ROUTINE: CONNECTING WITH FAMILIES, GROUPS, TEAMS, AND TRIBES

We are social creatures. We are born into or choose to belong to partners, families, teams, and communities. The more stressed we feel, the more we divide the world into "us" and "them." Although these groups can be the source of much stress, belonging to them is essential to renewal.

The simple act of eating meals with people you trust goes well beyond whatever words are spoken. Eye contact, tone of voice, facial expressions, and even the action of swallowing connect our nervous systems in ways that calm the stress autopilot and trigger renewal. Doing those things stimulates your vagus nerve, whose activation, as you'll recall, improves resilience by quieting your autopilot. Looking others in the eye, touching by shaking hands or hugging, eating together, speaking in calm tones—all of these deliver unspoken messages that tell your brain and body that it is safe to activate renewal.

Group activities with synchronized movements and breathing, such as exercise classes, sports, dance, drumming, music performance, and yoga, even though they may be physically challenging, can have the same effect, triggering renewal and growth. Even gossip, as poisonous as it is in the long run, bonds people by saying that "we" are not like "them."

Kurt Hahn, creator of Outward Bound, described the adventure program as a "double-edged sword" that first cuts people then heals them stronger than before. Social support has always been an essential part of Outward Bound's philosophy and approach. James T. Neill, an educational psychologist who tested the idea that the program's challenges resulted in greater resilience, not only found that it did so but that social support was crucial.[30] Interestingly, he found that the best predictor of increased resilience was the perceived support of the *least* supportive group member.

ROUTINE: HUMOR

When I meet children in the aftermath of high stress and trauma, I give out Junior Firefighter badge stickers. Kids love them. Their parents are usually around, so as I give the children stickers, I sometimes say, "This will get you out of speeding tickets!" Everybody usually laughs and some of the tension melts away.

Humor helps. It feeds the good wolf, helping us regain lost perspective and take a break from negativity and darkness even at the worst of times, when used appropriately. I'm not suggesting that you turn off your sensitivity during suffering. Black humor is common in public safety, but it belongs behind our own closed doors. As a former Marine told me, "Dark humor is like clean drinking water—not everybody gets it." The risk of dark humor is that it feeds cynicism, the enemy of optimism.

Humor bonds friendships and marriages, helping us laugh at ourselves and whatever life might toss at us. Silliness has the power to balance some of life's seriousness. Flexibility is a trait of resilient people; what could be more flexible than to laugh in the face of trauma?

My friend Dave, who lost a child to a brain tumor and then later developed one himself (totally unrelated, just an awful coincidence), rarely lost his sense of humor. Some of the "tumor humor" was dark, even morbid. Dave on his brain surgery: "I needed that like I needed a hole in the head." "I gave those doctors a piece of my mind." And so on. (Although a child's life-threatening illness is often called every parent's worst nightmare, most certainly a high-stress event, parents of children with cancer report no more posttraumatic stress than most people; they are *more likely* to experience posttraumatic growth![31])

Not taking yourself too seriously—your opinions, thoughts, and feelings—makes a difference. I've mostly extracted myself from the temptation to comment on politics in social media by reminding myself that I'm just one voter without any special knowledge about 99 percent of the topics people fight about. These days, even I don't care much what I think! When I do have some expertise, I'll do my best to speak up, as objectively as possible, letting go of any expectation of changing anyone else's mind. If they do, great, but I'm not going to insist. That would be an "unenforceable rule," which I'll cover in the next chapter.

Laugh at yourself too. All of us are a bit ridiculous.

ROUTINE: COMPANION ANIMALS

Growing scientific evidence supports what we already knew about companion animals—their unconditional attachment reminds us that we are not alone and helps us cope. Dogs and horses are especially sensitive to our emotions and state of mind. Our nervous systems connect with them through the same sensory and hormone feedback loops that help tense people relax in the presence of one who is calm. Eye contact, body language, touch, and other interactions raise the levels of renewal hormones in pets and people.

Crisis and therapy dogs are making a substantial difference in the way we support public safety employees. In 2015, during large wildland fires in California, several fire chaplains brought along their personal service dogs. We noticed that firefighters, most of whom would walk quickly past the peer support trailer, stopped to play with the dogs. Fast-forward to the more recent huge fires—dog teams have been at nearly all large fire camps. Cal Fire and others have partnered with organizations such as Hope Animal-Assisted Crisis Response and K-9 First Responders.

I went to Las Vegas with K-9 First Responders as a follow-up to the horrendous Route 91 mass shooting that killed fifty-eight people and wounded 422. I joined Spartacus, a 125-pound Akita, and his handler, executive director Brad Cole, to check in with firefighters. I came along to learn more about how and why dogs can be so effective.

> There is nothing either good or bad but thinking makes it so.
>
> **—WILLIAM SHAKESPEARE**

The comments were consistent—dogs can always tell when you've had a difficult day. Since they can't talk, they won't try to change you or make you feel better. They don't cry; they just accompany you. Even though they can tell we are upset, they don't take on our feelings. That's a wonderful example of social support. Dogs *accept* us as just as we are.

I don't have as much firsthand experience with horses—we co-own an American quarter horse, Muñeca, but she definitely belongs to my wife. They can't go as many places as dogs, although I've seen pictures of a comfort horse making hospital visits!

Horses are smart and social, incredibly attuned to our state of mind. Equine therapy and equine coaching show impressive results and are worth looking into if you like horses and can imagine they would help you.

Dogs and horses have a significant difference. Dogs are predators, inclined more toward *fight* than flight. When a dog is friendly and senses that you are upset, it will come to you and respond to the emotions it senses. Horses, as prey animals, have more *flight* than fight, so they have an amazing ability to sense if you are calm. Horses will stay away until you become more centered and relaxed, which makes them excellent at giving you feedback about your state of arousal or calm.

Caring for any companion animal (or plant, for that matter) creates resilience. Pets that need regular exercise help motivate us to do the same, providing purpose and responsibility, satisfying some of our deep need for meaning.

ROUTINE: GIVING AND RECEIVING KNOWLEDGE AND WISDOM

Which teachers, coaches, or mentors are you most grateful for? Who has given you knowledge, the mental tools that allowed you to take on new challenges, to set your sights higher?

Earlier, I described how I learned cash-flow forecasting from my friend John Lemons, who was my first start-up investor and a business and finance mentor. One of John's most effective confidence builders—and I don't know if it was intentional or not—was that often when I felt desperate for guidance, he didn't call me back for several days. By the time he returned my call, I often had solved the problem on my own. I learned to trust my instincts and avoid passively waiting.

Generosity isn't just about money. Resilient people are also quicker to share their time and knowledge; they have a stronger sense of *interdependence*. They know that overcoming obstacles and seizing opportunities work best when many people invent and share new ways of making, understanding, and believing—sometimes for individual profit, sometimes for social return on investment. Life improves faster for everyone when we don't have to try to do everything for ourselves—physically, socially, and spiritually. On our own, we are quite limited. Self-sufficiency and interdependence are not opposites. In fact, each utterly requires the other. The greatest way we can increase our own resilience is by making those around us stronger and more resilient.[32]

Be a coach, mentor, or teacher.

the risks and rewards of caring

In this chapter, I've urged you to look for and nurture friendships and other social support. The risk you take when you create such bonds is that you will lose those people. Or worse, they may betray you. That's the price of caring and connecting.

The good news is that the more social support resources you have, the more resilient you will be when pain happens. As part of a larger, more bonded community, you'll experience more losses, and they'll hurt more than if you had kept your distance. But that same community is one of your greatest assets. The benefits far outweigh the risks.

> People experience the life-changing force of healing relationships when something powerful comes out of one and touches something good in another.
>
> **—LARRY CRABB**

When high stress hits, fight or flight is not the only potential reaction. We also have the tend and befriend instinct. It drives us to gather with family and friends to give and receive support when times are tough. This caring-oriented stress reaction makes us less selfish and more courageous. We gather with and protect those we care about, especially the most vulnerable. When you choose to help, you activate the tend-and-befriend stress reaction, reducing fear and increasing hope and optimism. I'll repeat—caring creates resilience.

It is uncomfortable to be in the presence of hurting people. As I often remind our crisis intervention team, when people sob or express other strong emotions, take it as an honor. It means they trust you.

> Grief and gratitude are kindred souls, each pointing to the beauty of what is transient and given to us by grace.
>
> **—DIANA BUTLER BASS**

spiritual resilience routines: connecting with beliefs

Look up is the *spiritual* reminder. There's more to life than survival, money, and power. Ethics, morals, and other values allow us to find and make meaning, set goals, have a mission and purpose. Know your values; share and teach them, especially by example. Know *why* you believe what you choose to believe and why you do what you choose to do. Spiritual routines have to do with values and goals. They help you develop, maintain, and share meaning, mission, and purpose.

Look up is the reminder that the universe is vaster than we can understand; that life can be more than just following selfish, survivalist instincts. Spirituality, in these pages, refers to values, principles, and meaning: your "whys," your motivations. These can be hard to hold onto; the world is full of shortcuts and other temptations that violate our values.

Many of us have found that belief in a higher power rings true, supplying comfort. Even if we don't feel in control, it is comforting and calming to have faith that someone or something has the universe under control. People with a stronger sense of purpose and meaning are happier and more hopeful. Spiritual resilience routines are about building your sense of purpose, choosing what you say yes to and why. Our beliefs change the way we interpret our lives, which can transform our automatic reactions.

God does not play dice with the universe.

—ALBERT EINSTEIN

Adding spiritual engagement is most important if you are a Helper, Achiever, or Romantic. You need to gain perspective to put your own needs in balance with the needs of others. Learn to see the bigger picture of how you fit into the world, what is or is not your responsibility or role. Become better at noticing when your selflessness is also selfish.

If you are a Challenger, Mediator, or Reformer, you are too rigid in your values, so you'll grow more flexible and resilient by increasing your spiritual renewal. "Pause and plan" will increase your ability to see when you are abusing your power and recognize when to let go of control.

When I talk about spiritual strength, I mean having beliefs and values, finding or making meaning out of even the greatest difficulties. Psychology considers purpose and meaning to be an important enough topic that the Purpose in Life survey, below, has been widely used in recent decades. Psychiatrist Viktor Frankl created it. He was a survivor of Nazi concentration camps and author of *Man's Search for Meaning,* an international best seller published in 1959. The survey asks questions about mood, goals, and the meaning of your life.

THE PURPOSE IN LIFE TEST

Score each question from 1 to 5 based on the part of the statement that is most true for you right now.

1. I am usually: bored (1); enthusiastic (5).
2. Life seems to me: completely routine (1); always exciting (5).
3. In life I have: no goals or aims (1); clear goals and aims (5).
4. My personal existence is: utterly meaningless, without purpose (1); purposeful and meaningful (5).
5. Every day is: exactly the same (1); constantly new and different (5).
6. If I could choose, I would: prefer to never have been born (1); want nine more lives just like this one (5).
7. After retiring, I would: loaf completely the rest of my life (1); do some of the exciting things I've always wanted to (5).
8. In achieving life goals I have: made no progress whatever (1); progressed to complete fulfillment (5).
9. My life is: empty, filled only with despair (1); running over with exciting things (5).
10. If I should die today, I'd feel that my life has been: completely worthless (1); very worthwhile (5).
11. In thinking of my life, I: often wonder why I exist (1); always see reasons for being here (5).
12. As I view the world in relation to my life, the world: completely confuses me (1); fits meaningfully with my life (5).
13. I am a: very irresponsible person (1); very responsible person (5).
14. Concerning freedom to choose, I believe humans are: completely bound by limitations of heredity and environment (1); totally free to make all life choices (5).

15. With regard to death, I am: unprepared and frightened (1); prepared and unafraid (5).
16. Regarding suicide, I have: thought of it seriously as a way out (1); never given it a second thought (5).
17. I regard my ability to find a purpose or mission in life as: practically none (1); very great (5).
18. My life is: out of my hands and controlled by external factors (1); in my hands and I'm in control of it (5).
19. Facing my daily tasks is: a painful and boring experience (1); a source of pleasure and satisfaction (5).
20. I have discovered: no mission or purpose in life (1); a satisfying life purpose (5).

Scoring: Add up all the scores for each item (20–100). A score of less than 50 may indicate that you are experiencing significant "existential concerns" in your life.

Research consistently finds that having a strong sense of purpose is part of being resilient for people of all ages. But purpose isn't fixed, it is a journey that changes, varying across times and parts of your life. Age makes a difference. If you are in your teens or twenties, it is normal to search for meaning and purpose. People who are older and still searching, however, are less content.[1]

Don't worry about nailing down your "one true purpose." Nobody has just one. In different areas of your life, and at various times, your purpose will vary. Purpose is not a destination; it is a journey and a way of living, something you cultivate by regularly wrestling with your priorities and goals. Spiritual stress—selfish and survivalist—is the urge to look out only for yourself and those you care most about. Like all stress responses, it is an important tool in your kit, helping you to "zoom in" on opportunities, challenges, and threats. Spiritual renewal allows you to get your perspective back, to gain sight of the bigger picture, and remember that caring for others and making the world a better place are also important.

> What you can plan is too small for you to live.
>
> —DAVID WHYTE

Psychological research shows that spirituality helps with depression and anxiety.[2] It can be a crucial part of recovery from self-destructive habits.[3]

Religion is a source, sometimes *the* source, of values and morality for many people. Religiousness is a predictor of posttraumatic growth, likely because a religious view of life makes it easier to find meaning in negative events.[4] I am a Christian and a fire chaplain, but in that role, I don't promote any religion or belief system. The chaplain's job is to be present to those undergoing hardship, offering comfort and hope, sometimes only as a symbol. That doesn't mean that I don't talk about beliefs if I'm asked. Even though I have more freedom to talk about my own faith when I'm not serving as a chaplain, I still operate on the conviction that attraction is far better than promotion and persuasion. Besides, being a chaplain, like any other support role, calls for far more listening than talking. Just showing up, confirming that you care, makes a difference, even if you say nothing at all.

routines for exercising your spiritual skills

Unlike rocks, plants, and animals, we humans are able to choose our priorities. Yet many of us, much of the time, do not stop and *decide* what is most important. If we don't choose, we will just react on autopilot to whatever the universe tosses our way.

Look at your calendar and financial statements. Where are you spending your time and money? What do you invest your thoughts in? Those are your current priorities. Are you satisfied with them?

If not, use your imagination to come up with new possibilities and dreams. Apply your intelligence to think and plan how you will make your choices into actual priorities.

You'll know that you have chosen authentic priorities when you see that they fit your mission and values, when you can feel that they give you motivation and energy. Authentic priorities free us from the forces of circumstance, others' expectations, and our own habits, helping us focus on our true selves.

Priorities, like everything else that contributes to resilience, need to be realistically optimistic—based in hope, joined to reality. If you are spending all of your time outside of your comfort zone, an examination of your priorities is a good way to decide what you'll let go.

As I've repeated, all resilience routines build and maintain connections, relationships of grateful receiving and generous giving. In the spiritual domain, we *receive* wisdom about values, meaning, and purpose from sacred, wise, and inspirational writings and people. We *give* by living out our mission and values, showing and teaching others the same.

ROUTINE: EXPERTISE AND INTERESTS

Knowing and developing expertise and interests will help you identify and pursue purpose. This is identity building; the more solidly you know who you are, the more purposeful you can become. Once again, resilience shows up as realistic optimism: knowing who you are is realistic, having a strong sense of purpose is optimistic.

ROUTINE: BUILDING YOUR VISION, MISSION, AND INSPIRATION

Why do you do what you do? What is your purpose? Where are you headed? It is fine if your answers to these kinds of questions stay fluid. But if you can't answer them at all, you'll have a tough time being resilient. Without a sense of mission, a strong personal *why*, we have a tough time setting goals, staying focused, and coming back from adversity.

Where does inspiration, vision, and mission come from? The answer is the same three dimensions I've been talking about: connecting to and nurturing your physical, social, and spiritual relationships, while avoiding getting stuck in a rut, any rut. The physical world can inspire you, from the majesty of a solar eclipse to the wonder of billions of transistors squeezed onto the microchips that power computers and phones. The selflessness and kindness of people and pets, as well as books, videos, art, music, and other creations, can inspire us. The word *inspiration* also means "to breathe"—recall the way that breathing can activate renewal. Some believe that all inspiration comes from a higher power, such as the Christian belief that the Holy Spirit (*pneuma,* meaning "air") is the source of all inspiration.

> Why, sometimes I've believed as many as six impossible things before breakfast.
>
> **—THE RED QUEEN IN *THROUGH THE LOOKING-GLASS*,**
> **LEWIS CARROLL**

I doubt if anyone has ever been tired and inspired, so if you seek inspiration, that is yet another reason to sleep long and well. Sleep has also been associated with creativity—your brain puts things together in new ways as you sleep and helps you remember them.[5]

ROUTINE: CHOOSING, KNOWING, AND LIVING YOUR VALUES

Connecting to personal values can make you more resilient by helping reduce the sense that you are threatened by information that contradicts your beliefs,[6] lessening how much you ruminate on failure,[7] and diminishing defensiveness.[8] In laboratory research, reflecting on personal values reduced stress responses, lowering cortisol levels; the effect was strongest for those with a positive view of their personal resources.[9] These studies are especially relevant to the COVID-19 pandemic because they specifically looked at people's resistance to believing important health information.

Here are some ways to choose and connect more strongly to values:

- Get creative. Draw, with an app or good old pen and paper. You might also cut out magazine pictures that represent your values. Use presentation software to create a slide show that illustrates your values with images, text, or whatever else works for you. Keep it general—this is not about specific goals, which should flow from your values.
- Discuss. Talk with friends, mentors, and other social supporters about your values. If you did the step above, "show and tell" what it was like to create it.
- Consider something in your life that is challenging you now. Write a short description of it. Think about why it is worthwhile to get through it. Make a list of as many reasons as you can. Now consider your personal values, the ones that make it worth persevering. Don't worry about getting anything exactly correct; your goal is to identify the values that resonate with your reasons for getting through the challenge.
- Make yourself a visual reminder of your values. Put it somewhere you'll see it regularly.
- Use the list below to help you think of values that matter to you.

I've talked about four values that are essential to resilience—gratitude, generosity, optimism, and realism. What else do you value most? Below is a list. I invite you to select two or three to prioritize. Follow your heart. Consider what you are passionate about, what you like and dislike.

> Chasing meaning is better for your health than trying to avoid discomfort.
>
> —KELLY MCGONIGAL

WHAT ARE YOUR CORE VALUES?

This list can get you started if you've never explored your personal values.

Acceptance	Compassion
Accountability	Competence
Achievement	Competition
Action	Completion
Advancement	Connectedness
Adventure	Consistency
Affection	Cooperation
Altruism	Country
Arts	Courage
Authenticity	Creativity
Awareness	Decisiveness
Balance	Democracy
Beauty	Dependability
Boldness	Design
Calmness	Discovery
Challenge	Diversity
Change	Economic Security
Collaboration	Education
Community	Effectiveness

Efficiency

Elegance

Empathy

Enlightenment

Entertainment

Enthusiasm

Environmental

Equality

Ethics

Excellence

Excitement

Exhilaration

Experiment

Expertise

Fairness

Faith

Fame

Family

Fast Pace

Freedom

Friendship

Frugality

Fun

Grace

Growth

Happiness

Harmony

Health

Helping Others

Helping Society

Honesty

Humility

Humor

Imagination

Improvement

Independence

Individuality

Influencing Others

Inner Harmony

Innovation

Inspiration

Integrity

Intelligence

Intuition

Involvement

Kindness

Knowledge

Leadership

Learning

Loyalty

Magnificence

Making a Difference

Mastery

Meaningful Work

Ministering

Modesty

Money

Morality

Mystery

Nature

Open-Mindedness

Order

Originality

Passion

Peace

Personal Development

Personal Expression

Planning

Play

Pleasure

Power	Sexuality
Privacy	Sincerity
Professionalism	Sophistication
Promotion	Spark
Purity	Speculation
Quality	Spirituality
Radiance	Stability
Recognition	Status
Relationships	Success
Religion	Teaching
Reputation	Tenderness
Respect	Thrill
Responsibility	Tradition
Risk Safety & Security	Trust
Self-Respect	Unity
Sensibility	Variety
Sensuality	Wealth
Serenity	Winning
Service	Wisdom

Revisit your values as you grow and get to know yourself better. You'll find many exercises and books available to help you go deeper to discover and choose your core values. Remember, an effect of your spiritual stress reaction is tunnel vision, loss of perspective. A personal vision statement can help you escape that trap, by reminding you of what was important before crisis struck.

ROUTINE: SETTING GOALS

Creating a mission statement and naming your core values naturally leads into goals. You need goals. You can't know what to hope or dream for without a clear sense of direction. How will you carry out the mission you've chosen? How will you know when you get there?

164 ■ **STRESS INTO STRENGTH**

I said this earlier, but it bears repeating—goals need to be optimistic and realistic. Stretch too far and you'll easily become discouraged. Stick only to what you are confident you can do, and you'll never discover your true limits.

renewal from spiritual stress

PRACTICING GRATEFULNESS AND GENEROSITY

Small habits of pausing and planning for gratefulness and generosity will help you to regain the perspective that spiritual stress takes away. If you build your gratitude and generosity, I assure you that you will be surprised and pleased by the results. These practices help build the important resilience habit of optimism.

ROUTINE: GRATEFULNESS AND ANONYMOUS KINDNESS

Get yourself a notebook or pad. For thirty days, which don't have to be in a row (remember, *start small and give yourself unlimited permission to fail and start over*), write down three things you are grateful for and three things you are looking forward to. Each day, do one *anonymous* act of kindness. These things can be small or large. You might be grateful for something as small as someone allowing you to merge into traffic in front of you— and your act of generosity could be to do the same for someone else. If you are in a position to do so and it seems right, do something big—fund a scholarship for a student, make a large donation to a charity. Whatever you do, *no one can ever know about it except you.*

One of the things that anonymous giving teaches us is the difference between being nice and being kind, which I mentioned earlier. Remember, when we are nice, it usually is so that others will like us. When we are kind, we give gifts that cannot be repaid.

ROUTINE: NOTICING AND LETTING GO OF UNENFORCEABLE RULES

I've warned repeatedly about the dangers of should-ing on yourself. I know that they are difficult to release. Shoulds can be things that happen even though you believe they *should not*—abuse, neglect, cheating, violence, illness, and even trivial things like drivers who tailgate (whom I have trouble forgiving). They can also be things that you believe *should* happen, but do not—acceptance, love, forgiveness, job promotion, success.

Frederic Luskin, author of *Forgive for Good,* describes what happens when we allow a should too much space in our heads. He calls it a grievance, signaled by thinking more about it than the good things, discomfort when you think about it, repetitive thoughts or repeating the same "grievance story" to companions over and over.

Grievances arise when we hold onto what Luskin has aptly named "unenforceable rules"—his name for the shoulds. I invite you to name your unenforceable rules and talk about them with trusted supportive people. Luskin has had extraordinary success in helping people work through seemingly unforgivable pain. Here is what he has observed about getting stuck:

- You take offense too personally.
- You blame the offender for how you feel.
- You create a grievance story featuring you as the victim.

When you have unenforceable rules, forgiveness can feel impossible or undeserved. If this is where you find yourself, realize that forgiveness is a *process,* not a just a decision. Most important, forgiveness *has nothing to do with the person who hurt you.* Let go of the idea that you cannot forgive someone unless they are sorry. Forgiveness is about freeing *you* from the burden of your anger and resentments.

Luskin's process of forgiveness includes the three elements above:

- Recognize that whoever hurt you did it for reasons that may be personal but are also impersonal. Bear in mind that "hurt people hurt people" or, if you prefer, "if they were raised by wolves, they're gonna bite."
- Let go of blaming. Accountability is proper, but repayment, punishment, or other consequences differ from continuing to blame others for your struggles.
- Discover that your version of the grievance story is not the whole story. Share your story with your social supporters—your "board of directors," a life coach, pastor, or therapist. Listen to what they heard you say. This is a time to ask for advice. This is a chance to rewrite your story.

When we let go of unenforceable rules, we transform pain from *betrayal* into *disappointment*. Betrayals are unacceptable; turning them into disappointments builds up your essential resilience trait of *acceptance*. Acceptance does not mean approval; it means showing up and remaining present rather than allowing your stress reactions to rule by fighting or giving up.

I came to the Bay Area Critical Incident Stress Management Team as a client after our niece's husband, USMC Lance Corporal Wes Canning, was killed in action in Fallujah, Iraq. For many years, I was unwilling to even think about forgiving whoever blew him to bits. I felt guilty, imagining I *should* be able to forgive anything, since I'm a Christian and, for goodness sakes, I'm a chaplain!

Luckily, I've learned to be gentle with myself (that's a motto of our CISM Team) and gave myself permission to set forgiveness aside indefinitely. God can forgive him, I told friends—I don't even want to think about him. It felt like I'd be betraying our niece and Wes's family. That's the myth that forgiveness would mean approval of bad behavior. It's not. But I was also caring too much what others would think of me if I forgave his killer.

> When we choose forgiveness we release our past to heal our present.
>
> **—FREDERIC LUSKIN**

Everything changed one weekend. For twenty-five years I've taken part regularly in a four-day Christian retreat called the Walk to Emmaus. Starting with my very first, the retreat has created times and places for me to let go of some of my deepest pain.

During my first Emmaus weekend, as a "new pilgrim," I spoke aloud for the first time about how much my father's criticism, anger, and violence hurt. On another retreat, I confessed how angry I felt that my best friend's young son had suffered and died. That's all I was going to say, but more words came to me: "And I know it's because I don't understand." As I spoke, surrounded by some of the best friends a man could have, I felt a huge weight vanish. I had never put much stock in the idea of instant healing; it always seemed as though something that could go away in a moment could come back just as fast. But now I know it happens.

Fourteen years after Wes was killed, at an Emmaus service of confession and healing, I realized that it was time to let go of more grievances (terrific young men like Wes *should not* die; people *should not* kill other people; our leaders *should not* manipulate evidence to justify war[10]) and that it was also time to speak words of forgiveness, from my heart, for the enemy who fired a rocket-powered grenade at him on November 10, 2004. I knew that Wes's killer also died that day; his crew chief told me that Marines leveled the building from which he had fired the rocket.

I told the men at the retreat that it was time for me to stop carrying the anger and resentments because none of that was good for me. I was stuck, just as Luskin describes.

Here's the part of this story that can still bring me to tears. A Marine, a veteran of the Iraq war, who was attending his first retreat as a "new pilgrim," came up to me afterwards and thanked me with a big hug. But his thanks had nothing to do with the Marine Corps or the war. He said I'd helped him realize how much he needed to forgive someone who had wounded him deeply. Later, I learned that the "someone" was his father, who had abandoned his family.

> Doing an injury puts you below your enemy; Revenging one makes you but even with him; Forgiving it sets you above him.
>
> **—BENJAMIN FRANKLIN**

Let me be clear that I'm okay with it taking me fourteen years to get to the place where I could forgive. Luskin writes that we cannot truly forgive until we acknowledge how deeply we've been hurt. That can take a long time, even a lifetime. And that's okay. Forgiving too soon—before you have acknowledged your deepest pain—can set you back a long way by burying your hurt even more deeply.

Forgiveness isn't only about others hurting us. We also need to forgive ourselves. I've said that guilt and shame are the biggest obstacles to resilience. They are chains that hold us back from coming home, even if home is a place we have never really known. Shame, the feeling that you aren't good or aren't good enough, will powerfully block healing and wholeness. To escape those chains, I invite you to begin to become less critical, more compassionate, and more forgiving to yourself and others.

We can end up carrying guilt and shame when we excuse, minimize, or rationalize pain caused by those closest to us: "It wasn't really that bad." "(S)he means well." "I deserved it." "X had it much worse than I did."

Admitting, even to yourself, how badly abuse or neglect has hurt you may be hard. Granting forgiveness can be extraordinarily difficult (and equally powerful). Don't be in a hurry. Remember that forgiveness is a decision *and* a process. I'll repeat, you cannot fully forgive someone until you have fully acknowledged the anger, pain, betrayal, and other emotions you felt. Realize this: virtually *everyone* who experienced childhood abuse or neglect enters adulthood telling themselves, "It wasn't that bad." Healing begins when you acknowledge, to those you trust, how bad it actually was for the child that you were at the time.

Neglect, especially emotional neglect, is one of the most difficult wounds to acknowledge. Abuse is hard, but when you have been abused, you know that something happened, even if you minimize the pain it caused. Neglect is tougher because it is an absence rather than an occurrence. Childhood emotional neglect leaves you homesick for a place you have never been. That is confusing.

If this is an important topic for you, I suggest reading *Forgive for Good* or watching Luskin's YouTube videos. His website is learningtoforgive.com.

As this book was nearing completion, I was assigned to the largest fire in California history, the August Complex. It was one of dozens of fires that broke out in Northern California during a lightning storm on August 16, 2020. As a result, we were extraordinarily shorthanded, lacking important equipment and services, stretched very thin. Everyone was tired and overwhelmed; I'm sure all, like me, worried what effect fatigue and stress would have on our safety. A firefighter from Texas, Diana Jones, was killed in an accident on our fire not long after I arrived; I heard all of the sobering radio traffic. In this environment, we have to hold in a lot of emotions so that we can do our work without distraction. Yet they always come out in some way. To my great surprise, in the midst of this long, long firefight, for the first time in my life, I felt an urge to write poetry. This seems like the right place to offer it.

REMEMBER

This is not for anyone except you.
This is not about anyone except you.

Take a moment. Just a moment.
Remember not hating your enemies.
Remember accepting disagreement over desire for destruction.
Remember understanding and respect.

Your heart remembers when certainty and outrage did not own you. Stop by.
Even for a millisecond, return to your true home. Grow hungry to be free of the chains of being right.

Your soul has always known that service and sacrifice bond us infinitely deeper than chains of agreement or domination. Problem-solving is only one path.
For one entire second, park your bulldozer. Recall why you own chains. Everything feels heavy when you hold them tightly.

Your troubled past is a whispered demand: Hold tightly to these lessons.
Your blessed future invites: Open your hand.

Become small now and then. Shrivel the magnificent fears of helplessness. How big is your life? Your God?

You have been there. Recall, even briefly, living free of deadly outrage and certainty.
Remember why you own chains. Take a moment. Just a moment. Remember.
Recall being you.
In your true home you are truly alive.

ROUTINE: SELF-COMPASSION

Self-compassion is a strong antidote to blame and shame, whether it comes from within you or outside. Compassion is the urge to accompany, comfort, and help those who are suffering, and there is no suffering we feel more than our own! Yet we often lack compassion for ourselves. We go "comparison stress shopping," minimizing our own distress because someone else's seems worse.

Aim to have as much compassion for yourself as you would for a friend in the grip of the inner critic. Imagine that your friend or loved one has gone through the same difficulties as you have. What would you say? By now I hope you understand that shoulds are off the table. A compassionate response sounds like this: "You were doing the best you could with what you had." Try telling *yourself* that. Give yourself a break, time to renew and heal.

Choose to believe, in your gut, that *you* have always been doing the best you can with what you had at the time. Yes, you can do better in the future, but accept yourself exactly as you are right now, instead of as a part of you thinks you *should* be. That's self-compassion. Remember, *life is hard.*

You'll easily find more information and courses in self-compassion. Research shows positive results from self-compassion education—better sleep, reduced anxiety and depression, and greater overall resilience.

ROUTINE: GROWING YOUR TRUST AND FAITH

Without trust, we would be entirely on our own. Trying to do it all yourself—self-sufficiency—is tempting, especially if you have been threatened or hurt, but we can live more fully when we are trusting and interdependent. Examples abound: money is a shared agreement to trust that a piece of paper or metal is worth more than its intrinsic value; every time you pass through an intersection when the traffic light is green, you are trusting that cross traffic will obey the red light; we trust EMS and firefighters to rescue us from danger and medical emergencies; we trust 911 call takers and dispatchers to answer the phone quickly and send the right kind of help when we need it. Those are dramatic kinds of trust, but trust can be more mundane. We trust that food at the grocery store is safe and, if not healthy, at least not harmful.

Stress and trauma break down trust. On autopilot we are suspicious and cynical, especially about those we don't regard as in our own "tribe."

Doing crisis intervention, I regularly visit neighborhoods where few people trust the police or anyone else in authority. I don't know how they can feel safe. I've been heartbroken to hear teachers tell me of poor children going hungry because their parents are so distrustful of authority that they won't fill out the paperwork for the school's lunch program. Without trust, we are on our own—an autopilot activator—far too much.

I'm not suggesting that you trust everyone. Have boundaries! Total vulnerability violates the "realistic" part of being realistically optimistic. Take notice of your own distrust and *choose* where to put your trust, based on your thoughts as well as the emotions that your autopilot drives.

Sometimes we need to trust without evidence. That's when faith comes in. Whether or not you believe in any kind of higher power, building trust requires stepping out in faith, because at the end of the day, the only way to build trust is to choose to be vulnerable and see what happens. Sometimes you'll find that you have misplaced your trust. But I can tell you from experience that taking a chance with a trustworthy friend or group by truly "getting real" can open the door to deep peace and joy.

Our negative bias is constantly ready to make us pessimistic. Since we cannot ever be certain of what the future holds, faith alone tells us that our troubles are temporary, not permanent. Without faith, sometimes the future looks dim indeed.

Rebuilding trust after grief and loss or especially after betrayal or other trauma takes time. Be patient and gentle with yourself. If your rope breaks while mountain climbing, it is only natural to distrust the next rope! You may need to go back to smaller, safer climbs and work your way back up to where you were before.

resilience after trauma

Excessive stress can injure us, physically, mentally, or spiritually. This is trauma. Like a physical injury, mental or spiritual trauma require time and rest to heal. You may need help and accommodations. Some injuries never heal completely—they leave scars or disabilities. Resilience after trauma does not mean that you will bounce back to the same place you were. Often, your life changes forever; you recover to a new normal. But that doesn't mean you can't bounce back to a good place.

Although physical trauma is inevitable if your body is subjected to extreme forces, mental and spiritual trauma are not as predictable. I might suffer a traumatic injury from an experience that was nothing more than highly stressful for you. Resilience routines can help make the difference between experiencing life events as traumatic versus stressful.

Everyone has limits. Practicing resilience routines doesn't guarantee that you won't face events that set off a threat reaction and make your stress autopilot stick. Terrible things happen to people every day. Life is hard! But psychological trauma results from your reaction, not what happened. (If that sounds like "it's your own fault," remember that we have limited control of our stress reactions.) People react differently to the same circumstances—an

event can be extremely traumatic for one person and not traumatic at all for another. There is no such thing as a "traumatic
incident," only "*potentially* traumatic" incidents.

For example, if someone collapses in front of you and you don't
have first aid and CPR training, you are likely to feel helpless and
out of control. If the same thing happens in front of me, I'll feel
high stress, but I will be confident that I can cope, thanks to my
training, experience, and equipment. I also know that if I fail to
save that person's life, it may be difficult emotionally, but I know
that I have resources for that, too, because they've been there for
me in the past.

Psychological "trauma" isn't well defined, but you can think of
it as a high-stress experience that changes you, leaving emotional
scars. In general, trauma results from situations that remind you,
in your gut, that you are fragile, meat and bones that other people,
accidents, or natural events can maim and kill.

Trauma can result from a onetime event, from which you may
recover relatively easily. When trauma is ongoing, however—
abuse, combat, and other stress that goes on for weeks, months,
or years—it is more difficult to heal.

Even a single-event trauma can take decades to heal if we stuff
down our reactions. For me, that was true of several things that
happened when I was in my twenties. I don't know if I have ever
really worked through the death of John Heidish, my firefighter
friend who died in a structure fire. A car crash in the middle of
the night at Yellowstone National Park, in which the victims uncannily resembled me (remember that *identification* amplifies
your stress response), took a lot of work—talking, writing, retriev-
ing the records.

Although I hesitate to declare that any single incident was the
worst I've experienced, the Easter Sunday fire mishap on Pittsburgh's South Side, which I described in the section on the myth
of stress as weakness, was one of the toughest to process. For
about five years after my friend Dave opened my eyes to the connection with the 9/11 images, I talked about it and wrote about

it, yet I still could barely address it without feeling overwhelmed. I even talked with the victim's son, whom firefighters had rescued minutes before I arrived (which I didn't know until I dug up newspaper accounts).

Eventually, out of frustration at my slow progress, I turned to a former paramedic, Karen Goehring, who is now a therapist for first responders and works with our CISM team. Karen guided me through eye movement desensitization and reprocessing (EMDR), which I mentioned earlier as the basis for "tapping" relaxation techniques. With Karen, I discovered feelings of responsibility and guilt that I didn't even suspect, thinking I was "just" a witness, not a participant. I felt as though I were part of the failure and guilty that I did nothing for those directly involved, even though, in those days, we had no idea what we could do.

After working with Karen, I was better but soon discovered that I had more to work on—and was impatient and angry with myself for still struggling to talk about the incident without tears. Eventually, months later, I found the courage to follow our team leader's suggestion to write letters to the two firefighters who were directly involved in the rescue. A lot of emotion poured into those words. When I finished, I realized I didn't need to send the letters, I just needed to write them. Today, as Karen promised, the memory is no longer a ghost that haunts me. Now it rests in a grave that I visit when I choose.

when to seek more help

As a crisis interventionist, I address only the immediate aftermath of potentially traumatic events. Often, I can do quite a bit to help people bounce back faster, reducing the duration of their suffering. The vast majority of people recover well from trauma, but sometimes we need more help—professional counseling or therapy.

Not all clinicians are trauma experts. When considering professionals, ask if their practice is "trauma informed." If not, find someone else. Also realize that it's important to "click" with counselors and therapists. If it's not working with the first one, try another. And another. If you get to five or six and nobody is clicking, perhaps you're just not ready.

The two biggest indications that it might be time to turn to a professional are isolation and helplessness. If you find that you are withdrawing from your normal social interactions or if you feel overwhelming helplessness or sadness—and those go on for weeks—seek expert support.

Other signs that you could benefit from working with a clinician or counselor include:

- You can't stop thinking about the trauma.
- You are unable to solve personal issues despite support and advice from people you trust.
- Sleep has been difficult for weeks or longer.
- You can't concentrate on work or everyday activities the way you used to.
- Your negative bias stays firmly in charge—you're always worried, irritable, angry, suspicious, and all the other bad wolf characteristics.
- You are struggling with substance abuse.
- An important relationship is in trouble.
- You are harming yourself or others or feel like you really might do so.
- You no longer do hobbies or the other things you enjoy.
- Friends report any of these behaviors, even though you aren't aware of them.

Spiritual trauma is also called *moral injury*: "perpetrating, failing to prevent, bearing witness to, or learning about acts that transgress deeply held moral beliefs and expectations." Journalist and poet Diane Silver has described moral injury as "a deep soul wound that pierces a person's identity, sense of morality, and relationship to society." Moral injury differs from other kinds of

trauma. If you are struggling with something that fits the definition, seek help from someone who understands and has specific
experience with it.

There's one more reason to see a therapist or counselor: to
make a good life even better. A regular mental health checkup is
not a bad idea. Life coaches, although they are not formally con-
sidered mental health professionals, can help you discover priorities, set goals, and develop and carry out other resilience routines.

Many trauma-informed therapists use EMDR to help you process past events. When it works, it is much faster than talk therapy. EMDR is so amazing that at the West Coast Posttrauma
Retreat for first responders, they hand out buttons that say "FM,"
which stands for "F—ing Magic," to describe the combination of
EMDR and other therapies that transform lives, restoring hope
and joy.

Always remember that *you* are the expert on your own life.

flashbacks, dissociation, and triggers

Trauma can result in *flashbacks, triggers,* or *dissociation* that get in
the way of building and keeping up your resilience.

During a flashback, you can feel and sometimes even think
that you are back in the traumatic event.

Dissociation is when you "space out," have the "thousand-yard
stare," or otherwise check out of the present. There's a bit more
to the specific psychological definition, but the important aspect
is that dissociation is the opposite of being present.

Triggers are reminders that bring up past traumatic injuries, producing the same feelings you had when the original trauma happened—fear, helplessness, extreme anxiety, and so forth. Sometimes
the reminder is obvious, such as when you retell the story of the
trauma or when you hear, see, or read a similar story. Others may
be sensory: a sight, smell, sound, or touch. There are time triggers:
anniversaries or events such as holidays. Others, often the most

powerful, are social: feeling unaccepted, disrespected, ignored, or unneeded. The 9/11 images were triggers for me.

I encourage you to begin noticing when you are triggered. Sometimes, even though you can tell you're triggered because you feel upset, it's hard to see what the trigger was. Be patient, give yourself time, and insight will come. Often, talking to a trusted supporter can help you discover what was going on. Resilience routines will help.

When you realize you're triggered, acknowledge it. I'm often triggered in my crisis intervention work because I'm constantly exposed to others' trauma. That results in "secondary trauma"—I can often feel some of what my clients are feeling, Empathy makes me good at this work, but it also leaves me vulnerable.

Physical resilience routines can help you make your way through triggers, flashbacks, and dissociation. Breathing, grounding, tapping—I use all of them on occasion.

These days, thanks to everything I do to stay resilient, when I'm triggered, all I usually need to do is acknowledge it to myself ("Okay, that was a trigger") and take a deep breath. But I also tell my team or some of my social support network. Sometimes when I speak, I discover that there was more to the trigger than I allowed myself to feel.

Demand for "trigger warnings" has become popular in some communities. The idea is that warnings should precede any material that might be triggering. There is scant evidence that these are helpful. When I'm significantly triggered, I "reframe" it as a positive, a signal that I need to do some more work on past trauma. The desire to avoid bad feelings is understandable, but it can easily turn into avoiding fully living.

High-stress, traumatic events leave us with complicated emotions: anger, grief, sadness, frustration, helplessness, and many others. Those around us often also want the "bad" feelings to go away too. We are uncomfortable around people having strong trauma-related emotions. Even though we have an amazing ability to distract or numb ourselves, stuffing down or hiding these reactions, they are still there. Nobody has figured out a way to let them go except by talking, sweating, and/or crying them out.

It is natural not to want to feel bad. "Why go back and talk about all that?" cops, firefighters, EMTs, and other public safety people often will ask me. We imagine that opening up will be worse than holding it all in. But in the long run, it's like what Shrek says about farting—"Better out than in."

Once again, I want to give you permission—*encourage* you—to be gentle with yourself. If you aren't ready to talk about difficult things, you aren't ready. Don't should on yourself (or anyone else) about it. You need to be in the right place, with the right person or people. Overdisclosing can be a mistake. Anyone who pressures you with phrases like "you need to talk about it, or you'll never get over it" only make things worse. Don't do that to others, either—*invite,* don't insist.

afterword

I'd like to set some expectations. I've urged you to stay connected physically to nature and your body, and although nature and bodies can be beautiful, they have messy, difficult, and even disgusting aspects. I've also urged you to stay connected socially. Human relationships also can be messy, difficult, and even disgusting. Spirituality, the third dimension of resilience, isn't all mountain-top experiences: you can't get to a mountain without passing through valleys.

In short, don't expect, or worse *demand,* that life become easier or more pleasant because you are building strength and resilience. If anything, I suspect it works the other way around. As we become more equipped to take on challenges, we face tougher stuff. For example, I would never have imagined that I could endure the secondary trauma of my work in crisis intervention. Yet I do (although I take breaks when I notice that it's getting to be too much).

If there's a "secret" to dealing with stress, grief, or trauma, it is to allow it to be more than one thing. My friend Dave looks back on losing his young son to brain cancer decades ago as a "bittersweet" time. Children suffering and dying is terrible. Friends and family coming together to support you is wonderful. It's not one or the other, it's both—a horrible privilege. Resilience routines are the same: difficult and discouraging at times, joyful and even euphoric at others. Let them be both.

I have gone back to locations of my most difficult critical incidents to add positive memories to the painful ones. My wife and I had a nice meal at a restaurant in Pittsburgh next to the building where the Easter Sunday incident took place. At Yellowstone National Park's gorgeous Fountain Flats, I took in the beauty of the meadows and forests, the bison herds and the sound of wolves howling in the distance, to let those memories accompany those of the night I was overwhelmed trying to care for multiple victims of a car crash that had disturbing personal connections. These good memories cannot erase the hard ones, but they accompany them, reminding me of what I'm grateful for.

Trauma can tempt us to go overboard to regain a sense of control. Physical strength tempts us to use force. Social strength tempts us toward tribalism, bigotry, and prejudice. Spiritual strength's temptation is self-righteousness.

Don't strive for "normal," which Carl Jung called "the ultimate aim of the unsuccessful."

If you have begun to grasp how essential physical, social, and spiritual connections are, you surely also are growing more aware of how disconnected our culture has become. Although that insight is discouraging, it also holds the seed of hope. I cannot imagine any kind of top-down, government, industry, or institutional initiative renewing the relationships that give us strength. I have developed a greater appreciation for the realistic optimism in Mother Teresa's instruction "Do small things with great love."

Choosing to do small things is realistic; doing them with great love is optimistic.

acknowledgments

I will always be grateful for the tremendous support I have received from family, friends, mentors, and clients. My wife, Cindy, has supported the disruptions to our lives that my work causes. She listens at least as well as our three dogs do. (That's a compliment; dogs are among the best listeners.) Janet Childs, founder of the Bay Area Critical Incident Stress Management Team and director of education at the Centre for Living with Dying, led me down this path and has been a comfort and inspiration to countless people, including me. I've had the privilege of training with Jeff Mitchell and George Everly, founders of the International Critical Incident Stress Foundation, the pioneers of modern crisis intervention. K-Love radio's free classes, through their Crisis Response Care program, connected me with other outstanding instructors: K. C. Peterson, Naomi Pagett, Tina Brooks, and Jennifer Ellers. Chief Jim Cook and the California Fire Chaplain Association helped me translate my skills into spiritual care and support. My home church for forty years, Bethel Lutheran in Cupertino, California, has been a rock; without support from its pastors, leaders, and congregation—along with Stephen Ministry and my other training—I can't imagine where I would be. Retreats and groups run by Walk to Emmaus, Broken Brothers, and our Illuman group, NorCal MALES (Men as Learners and Elders), along with Richard Rohr's leadership, have been amazing reservoirs of wisdom and support.

Cal Fire's Employee Support Services team, led in recent years by Bill Baxter, Bob Ellis, and Mike Ming, has been a privilege to work with. I am grateful to Davina Sentak for bringing me into ESS, and I'm always honored to be asked to serve. The same goes for Santa Clara County Parks and Supervising Ranger Aniko Milan, who were the test subjects for my first resilience training classes. A big thanks to Mike Hacke and Jerry Serpa, Spring Valley Fire Department chiefs, for inviting me on board and maintaining high standards of training and performance in cooperation with Cal Fire's Santa Clara Unit. The same is true for my wildland fire employers, the U.S. Forest Service and Wilderness Medics.

Three guys I regularly "get real" with, Dave Land, Dave Hibbert, and Bill Cole, have helped keep me sane by sharing a couple of thousand meals (continuing as Zoom meetings and socially distanced walks due to COVID-19) over the last few decades. I'm also grateful to my mentors, coaches, investors, and encouragers, especially Bruce Dobler, Tim Bajarin, John Lemons, Gary Kalus, and David Brin. Toastmasters taught me more than I expected, so a thank-you also to James Gardner for dragging me to the Early Risers meeting. Meanwhile, Margot Maley Hutchinson, my literary agent at Waterside Associates, has been a source of honest feedback and encouragement. And, I am always grateful to my parents, for choosing to live in a town with an outstanding public school system.

Please feel free to contact me. I welcome your feedback, corrections, and suggestions for improving future editions. You can find me on the Stress Into Strength Facebook page and YouTube channel, and on Twitter as @NickArnett.

notes

INTRODUCTION

1. By "spiritual," I am referring to meaning and values, distinct from religion, a source of spirituality.
2. The official name is the Arduous Work Capacity Test.
3. Dhabhar, Firdaus S. 2018. "The Short-Term Stress Response – Mother Nature's Mechanism for Enhancing Protection and Performance Under Conditions of Threat, Challenge, and Opportunity." *Frontiers in Neuroendocrinology*, Stress and the Brain, 49 (April): 175–92. https://doi.org/10.1016/j.yfrne.2018.03.004.
4. Dienstbier, Richard A. "Arousal and Physiological Toughness: Implications for Mental and Physical Health," 17.
5. Seery, Mark D., Raphael J. Leo, Shannon P. Lupien, Cheryl L. Kondrak, and Jessica L. Almonte. 2013. "An Upside to Adversity?: Moderate Cumulative Lifetime Adversity Is Associated With Resilient Responses in the Face of Controlled Stressors." *Psychological Science* 24 (7): 1181–89. https://doi.org/10.1177/0956797612469210.
6. Sudbrack, Roberto, Pedro H. Manfro, Isadora M. Kuhn, Hudson W. de Carvalho, and Diogo R. Lara. 2015. "What Doesn't Kill You Makes You Stronger and Weaker: How Childhood Trauma Relates to Temperament Traits." *Journal of Psychiatric Research* 62 (March): 123–29. https://doi.org/10.1016/j.jpsychires.2015.01.001; Santarelli, Sara, Christoph Zimmermann, Georgia Kalideris, Sylvie L. Lesuis, Janine Arloth, Andrés Uribe, Carine Dournes, et al. 2017. "An Adverse Early Life Environment Can Enhance Stress Resilience in Adulthood." *Psychoneuroendocrinology* 78 (April): 213–21. https://doi.org/10.1016/j.psyneuen.2017.01.021.
7. Masten, Ann S. 2014. *Ordinary Magic: Resilience in Development*. New York, US: Guilford Press.
8. Schaefer, Jeanne A., and Rudolf H. Moos. 1992. "Life Crises and Personal Growth." In *Personal Coping: Theory, Research, and Application*, 149–70. Westport, CT, US: Praeger Publishers/Greenwood Publishing Group.
9. Overmier, J. Bruce, and Martin E. Seligman. 1967. "Effects of Inescapable Shock upon Subsequent Escape and Avoidance Responding." *Journal of*

Comparative and Physiological Psychology 63 (1): 28–33. https://doi
.org/10.1037/h0024166.

10.   The dogs' failure to learn is likely because chronic stress interferes with mental coping by depleting adrenaline, a stress hormone that increases blood flow and glucose to the brain. Another stress hormone, noradrenaline, drives physical coping. As long as you don't run low, taking on challenges is likely to be enjoyable.

11.   Benjamin, Phyllis, and Joan Looby. 1998. "Defining the Nature of Spirituality in the Context of Maslow's and Rogers's Theories." *Counseling and Values* 42 (2): 92–100. https://doi.org/10.1002/j.2161-007X.1998.tb00414.x.

12.   This is the source of the name "beta blocker" for some medicines that lower high blood pressure.

13.   In your brain, the amygdala and limbic system.

14.   Taylor, Shelley E., Laura Cousino Klein, Brian P. Lewis, Tara L. Gruenewald, Regan A. R. Gurung, and John A. Updegraff. n.d. "Biobehavioral Responses to Stress in Females: Tend-and-Befriend, Not Fight-or-Flight," 64.

15.   Segerstrom, Suzanne C., Jaime K. Hardy, Daniel R. Evans, and Natalie F. Winters. 2012. "Pause and Plan: Self-Regulation and the Heart." In *How Motivation Affects Cardiovascular Response: Mechanisms and Applications*, 181–98. Washington, DC, US: American Psychological Association. https:// doi.org/10.1037/13090-009.

16.   Dhabhar, Firdaus S. 2009. "A Hassle a Day May Keep the Pathogens Away: The Fight-or-Flight Stress Response and the Augmentation of Immune Function." *Integrative and Comparative Biology* 49 (3): 215–36. https://doi .org/10.1093/icb/icp045.

17.   Cabo, Rafael de, and Mark P. Mattson. 2019. "Effects of Intermittent Fasting on Health, Aging, and Disease." *New England Journal of Medicine* 381 (26): 2541–51. https://doi.org/10.1056/NEJMra1905136.

18.   Wyngaarden, K. E. van, and E. K. J. Pauwels. 1995. "Hormesis: Are Low Doses of Ionizing Radiation Harmful or Beneficial?" *European Journal of Nuclear Medicine* 22 (5): 481–86. https://doi.org/10.1007/BF00839064.

19.   Pourshahidi, L. Kirsty, Luciano Navarini, Marino Petracco, and J. J. Strain. 2016. "A Comprehensive Overview of the Risks and Benefits of Coffee Consumption." *Comprehensive Reviews in Food Science and Food Safety* 15 (4): 671–84. https://doi.org/10.1111/1541-4337.12206.

20.   Rhee, Han van der, Esther de Vries, Claudia P. Coomans, Piet van de Velde, and Jan Willem W. Coebergh. 2016. "Sunlight: For Better or For Worse? A Review of Positive and Negative Effects of Sun Exposure." https://doi .org/10.17980/2016.156.

21.   Robinson, Matthew M., Surendra Dasari, Adam R. Konopka, Matthew L. Johnson, S. Manjunatha, Raul Ruiz Esponda, Rickey E. Carter, Ian R. Lanza, and K. Sreekumaran Nair. 2017. "Enhanced Protein Translation Underlies Improved Metabolic and Physical Adaptations to Different Exercise Training Modes in Young and Old Humans." *Cell Metabolism* 25 (3): 581–92. https://doi.org/10.1016/j.cmet.2017.02.009.

22.   Ristow, Michael, and Kim Zarse. 2010. "How Increased Oxidative Stress Promotes Longevity and Metabolic Health: The Concept of Mitochondrial Hormesis (Mitohormesis)." *Experimental Gerontology* 45 (6): 410–18. https://doi.org/10.1016/j.exger.2010.03.014.

23. Yerkes, Robert M., and John D. Dodson. 1908. "The Relation of Strength of Stimulus to Rapidity of Habit-Formation." *Journal of Comparative Neurology and Psychology* 18 (5): 459–82. https://doi.org/10.1002/cne.920180503.

24. Rimé, Bernard. 2009. "Emotion Elicits the Social Sharing of Emotion:) Theory and Empirical Review." *Emotion Review* 1 (January): 60–85. https://doi.org/10.1177/1754073908097189.

25. Petticrew, Mark P., and Kelley Lee. 2011. "The 'Father of Stress' Meets 'Big Tobacco': Hans Selye and the Tobacco Industry." *American Journal of Public Health* 101 (3): 411–18. https://doi.org/10.2105/AJPH.2009.177634.

26. Rosch, P. J. 1999. "Reminiscences of Hans Selye, and the Birth of 'Stress.'" *International Journal of Emergency Mental Health* 1 (1): 59–66.

27. Keller, Abiola, Kristin Litzelman, Lauren E. Wisk, Torsheika Maddox, Erika Rose Cheng, Paul D. Creswell, and Whitney P. Witt. 2012. "Does the Perception That Stress Affects Health Matter? The Association With Health and Mortality." *Health Psychology* 31 (5): 677–84. https://doi.org/10.1037/a0026743.

28. Felitti, Vincent J., Robert F. Anda, Dale Nordenberg, David F. Williamson, Alison M. Spitz, Valerie Edwards, Mary P. Koss, and James S. Marks. 1998. "Relationship of Childhood Abuse and Household Dysfunction to Many of the Leading Causes of Death in Adults: The Adverse Childhood Experiences (ACE) Study." *American Journal of Preventive Medicine* 14 (4): 245–58. https://doi.org/10.1016/S0749-3797(98)00017-8.

29. Farber, Madeline J., M. Justin Kim, Annchen R. Knodt, and Ahmad R. Hariri. 2019. "Maternal Overprotection in Childhood Is Associated with Amygdala Reactivity and Structural Connectivity in Adulthood." *Developmental Cognitive Neuroscience* 40 (December): 100711. https://doi.org/10.1016/j.dcn.2019.100711; Boyce, W. Thomas, and Bruce J. Ellis. 2005. "Biological Sensitivity to Context: I. An Evolutionary–Developmental Theory of the Origins and Functions of Stress Reactivity." *Development and Psychopathology* 17 (02). https://doi.org/10.1017/S0954579405050145.

30. Collins, Dave, and Áine MacNamara. 2012. "The Rocky Road to the Top." *Sports Medicine* 42 (11): 907–14. https://doi.org/10.1007/BF03262302.

31. Weststrate, Nic M., and Judith Glück. 2017. "Hard-Earned Wisdom: Exploratory Processing of Difficult Life Experience Is Positively Associated with Wisdom." *Developmental Psychology* 53 (4): 800–814. https://doi.org/10.1037/dev0000286; Bostock, Lucy, Alia I. Sheikh, and Stephen Barton. 2009. "Posttraumatic Growth and Optimism in Health-Related Trauma: A Systematic Review." *Journal of Clinical Psychology in Medical Settings* 16 (4): 281–96. https://doi.org/10.1007/s10880-009-9175-6.

CHAPTER 1

1. Johnson, Eric J., Simon Gaechter, and Andreas Herrmann. 2006. "Exploring the Nature of Loss Aversion." SSRN Scholarly Paper ID 892336. Rochester, NY: Social Science Research Network. https://papers.ssrn.com/abstract=892336.

2. Noakes, Timothy David. 2012. "Fatigue Is a Brain-Derived Emotion That Regulates the Exercise Behavior to Ensure the Protection of Whole Body Homeostasis." *Frontiers in Physiology* 3: 82. https://doi.org/10.3389/fphys.2012.00082.

3. "What Doesn't Kill You Makes You Stronger: Psychological Trauma and Its Relationship to Enhanced Memory Control." n.d. Accessed July 12, 2020. https://psycnet.apa.org/fulltext/2018-34715-001.html.

4. Lupien, Sonia J., Mony de Leon, Susan de Santi, Antonio Convit, Chaim Tarshish, N. P. V. Nair, Mira Thakur, Bruce S. McEwen, Richard L. Hauger, and Michael J. Meaney. 1998. "Cortisol Levels During Human Aging Predict Hippocampal Atrophy and Memory Deficits." *Nature Neuroscience* 1 (1): 69–73. https://doi.org/10.1038/271; Lupien, S., A. R. Lecours, I. Lussier, G. Schwartz, N. P. Nair, and M. J. Meaney. 1994. "Basal Cortisol Levels and Cognitive Deficits in Human Aging." *Journal of Neuroscience* 14 (5): 2893–2903. https://doi.org/10.1523/JNEUROSCI.14-05-02893.1994.

5. Takahashi, Taiki, Koki Ikeda, Miho Ishikawa, Takafumi Tsukasaki, Daisuke Nakama, Shigehito Tanida, and Tatsuya Kameda. 2004. "Social Stress-Induced Cortisol Elevation Acutely Impairs Social Memory in Humans." *Neuroscience Letters* 363 (2): 125–30. https://doi.org/10.1016/j.neulet .2004.03.062.

6. Jamieson, Jeremy P., Matthew K. Nock, and Wendy Berry Mendes. 2012. "Mind Over Matter: Reappraising Arousal Improves Cardiovascular and Cognitive Responses to Stress." *Journal of Experimental Psychology: General* 141 (3): 417–22. https://doi.org/10.1037/a0025719.

7. Pedersen, Cort A., Steven W.C. Chang, and Christina L. Williams. 2014. "Evolutionary Perspectives on the Role of Oxytocin in Human Social Behavior, Social Cognition and Psychopathology." *Brain Research* 1580 (September): 1–7. https://doi.org/10.1016/j.brainres.2014.07.033.

8. Lane, Anthony, Olivier Luminet, Bernard Rimé, James J. Gross, Philippe de Timary, and Moïra Mikolajczak. 2013. "Oxytocin Increases Willingness to Socially Share One's Emotions." *International Journal of Psychology* 48 (4): 676–81. https://doi.org/10.1080/00207594.2012.677540.

9. MacDonald, Kai, and Tina Marie MacDonald. 2010. "The Peptide That Binds: A Systematic Review of Oxytocin and Its Prosocial Effects in Humans." *Harvard Review of Psychiatry* 18 (1): 1–21. https://doi.org/10.3109 /10673220903523615.

10. Engert, Veronika, Anna M. Koester, Antje Riepenhausen, and Tania Singer. 2016. "Boosting Recovery Rather Than Buffering Reactivity: Higher Stress-Induced Oxytocin Secretion Is Associated with Increased Cortisol Reactivity and Faster Vagal Recovery After Acute Psychosocial Stress." *Psychoneuroendocrinology* 74 (December): 111–20. https://doi.org/10.1016/j .psyneuen.2016.08.029.

11. Gutkowska, J., and M. Jankowski. 2012. "Oxytocin Revisited: Its Role in Cardiovascular Regulation." *Journal of Neuroendocrinology* 24 (4): 599–608. https://doi.org/10.1111/j.1365-2826.2011.02235.x.

12. McEwen, Bruce S., and John H. Morrison. 2013. "The Brain on Stress: Vulnerability and Plasticity of the Prefrontal Cortex Over the Life Course." *Neuron* 79 (1): 16–29. https://doi.org/10.1016/j.neuron.2013.06.028.

13. Patrick, Vanessa M., and Henrik Hagtvedt. 2012. "'I Don't' Versus 'I Can't': When Empowered Refusal Motivates Goal-Directed Behavior." *Journal of Consumer Research* 39 (2): 371–81. https://doi.org/10.1086/663212.

14. Carrying *shoulds* for things that you cannot control is a recipe for frustration, anger, and resentment. More on the dangers of "unenforceable rules" later.

15. On YouTube, "Newhart Stop It."

CHAPTER 2

1. Pantell, Matthew, David Rehkopf, Douglas Jutte, S. Leonard Syme, John Balmes, and Nancy Adler. 2013. "Social Isolation: A Predictor of Mortality Comparable to Traditional Clinical Risk Factors." *American Journal of Public Health* 103 (11): 2056–62. https://doi.org/10.2105/AJPH.2013.301261.

2. Hallal, Pedro C., Lars Bo Andersen, Fiona C. Bull, Regina Guthold, William Haskell, Ulf Ekelund, and Lancet Physical Activity Series Working Group. 2012. "Global Physical Activity Levels: Surveillance Progress, Pitfalls, and Prospects." *Lancet* (London, England) 380 (9838): 247–57. https://doi.org/10.1016/S0140-6736(12)60646-1.

3. Hari, Johann. 2018. *Lost Connections: Uncovering the Real Causes of Depression - and the Unexpected Solutions.* Bloomsbury USA.

4. Sood, Amit. 2013. *The Mayo Clinic Guide to Stress-Free Living.* 1st edition. Cambridge, MA: Da Capo Lifelong Books.

5. Yao, Mike Z., and Zhi-jin Zhong. 2014. "Loneliness, Social Contacts and Internet Addiction: A Cross-Lagged Panel Study." *Computers in Human Behavior* 30 (January): 164–70. https://doi.org/10.1016/j.chb.2013.08.007.

6. Morahan-Martin, Janet, and Phyllis Schumacher. 2003. "Loneliness and Social Uses of the Internet." *Computers in Human Behavior* 19 (6): 659–71. https://doi.org/10.1016/S0747-5632(03)00040-2.

7. Bruce, Liana DesHarnais, Joshua S. Wu, Stuart L. Lustig, Daniel W. Russell, and Douglas A. Nemecek. 2019. "Loneliness in the United States: A 2018 National Panel Survey of Demographic, Structural, Cognitive, and Behavioral Characteristics." *American Journal of Health Promotion* 33 (8): 1123–33. https://doi.org/10.1177/0890117119856551.

8. Sanson, Mevagh, Deryn Strange, and Maryanne Garry. 2019. "Trigger Warnings Are Trivially Helpful at Reducing Negative Affect, Intrusive Thoughts, and Avoidance." *Clinical Psychological Science* 7 (4): 778–93. https://doi.org/10.1177/2167702619827018.

9. Obayashi, Konen. 2013. "Salivary Mental Stress Proteins." *Clinica Chimica Acta* 425 (October): 196–201. https://doi.org/10.1016/j.cca.2013.07.028.

10. Engert, Veronika, Anna M. Koester, Antje Riepenhausen, and Tania Singer. 2016. "Boosting Recovery Rather Than Buffering Reactivity: Higher Stress-Induced Oxytocin Secretion Is Associated With Increased Cortisol Reactivity and Faster Vagal Recovery After Acute Psychosocial Stress." *Psychoneuroendocrinology* 74 (December): 111–20. https://doi.org/10.1016/j.psyneuen.2016.08.029.

11. Kagerbauer, S. M., J. Martin, T. Schuster, M. Blobner, E. F. Kochs, and R. Landgraf. 2013. "Plasma Oxytocin and Vasopressin Do Not Predict Neuropeptide Concentrations in Human Cerebrospinal Fluid." *Journal of Neuroendocrinology* 25 (7): 668–73. https://doi.org/10.1111/jne.12038.

CHAPTER 3

1. This section is based on "The Four S's" by Dr. Lucinda Poole and Dr. Hugo Alberts.

2. Enneagram Type 8, also called the Boss or Leader.

3. Enneagram Type 9, also called the Peacemaker.

4. Enneagram Type 1, also called the Perfectionist.
5. Enneagram Type 2, also called the Giver.
6. Enneagram Type 3, also called the Performer.
7. Enneagram Type 4, also called the Individualist.
8. Enneagram Type 5, also called the Investigator or the Thinker.
9. Enneagram Type 6, also called the Loyalist, Trooper, or Devil's Advocate.
10. Enneagram Type 7, also called the Generalist or Epicure.

CHAPTER 4

1. Booth, Frank W., Christian K. Roberts, John P. Thyfault, Gregory N. Ruegsegger, and Ryan G. Toedebusch. 2017. "Role of Inactivity in Chronic Diseases: Evolutionary Insight and Pathophysiological Mechanisms." *Physiological Reviews* 97 (4): 1351–1402. https://doi.org/10.1152/physrev .00019.2016.
2. Knight, Joseph A. 2012. "Physical Inactivity: Associated Diseases and Disorders." *Annals of Clinical & Laboratory Science* 42 (3): 320–37.
3. Ding, Ding, Kenny D. Lawson, Tracy L. Kolbe-Alexander, Eric A. Finkelstein, Peter T. Katzmarzyk, Willem van Mechelen, and Michael Pratt. 2016. "The Economic Burden of Physical Inactivity: A Global Analysis of Major Non-Communicable Diseases." *Lancet* 388 (10051): 1311–24. https://doi .org/10.1016/S0140-6736(16)30383-X.
4. Bassett, David R. Jr, Holly R. Wyatt, Helen Thompson, John C. Peters, and James O. Hill. 2010. "Pedometer-Measured Physical Activity and Health Behaviors in U.S. Adults." *Medicine & Science in Sports & Exercise* 42 (10): 1819–1825. https://doi.org/10.1249/MSS.0b013e3181dc2e54.
5. Pratesi, Alessandra, Francesca Tarantini, and Mauro Di Bari. 2013. "Skeletal Muscle: An Endocrine Organ." *Clinical Cases in Mineral and Bone Metabolism* 10 (1): 11–14. https://doi.org/10.11138/ccmbm/2013.10.1.011.
6. Maiorana, Andrew, Gerard O'Driscoll, Roger Taylor, and Daniel Green. 2003. "Exercise and the Nitric Oxide Vasodilator System." *Sports Medicine* 33 (14): 1013–35. https://doi.org/10.2165/00007256-200333140-00001.
7. Srikanthan, Preethi, and Arun S. Karlamangla. 2011. "Relative Muscle Mass Is Inversely Associated With Insulin Resistance and Prediabetes. Findings from The Third National Health and Nutrition Examination Survey." *Journal of Clinical Endocrinology & Metabolism* 96 (9): 2898–2903. https://doi .org/10.1210/jc.2011-0435.
8. Adams, O Peter. 2013. "The Impact of Brief High-Intensity Exercise on Blood Glucose Levels." *Diabetes, Metabolic Syndrome and Obesity: Targets and Therapy* 6 (February): 113–22. https://doi.org/10.2147/DMSO.S29222.
9. Powers, Scott K., Li Li Ji, and Christiaan Leeuwenburgh. 1999. "Exercise Training-Induced Alterations in Skeletal Muscle Antioxidant Capacity: A Brief Review." *Medicine & Science in Sports & Exercise* 31 (7): 987–997.
10. Argilés, Josep M., Nefertiti Campos, José M. Lopez-Pedrosa, Ricardo Rueda, and Leocadio Rodriguez-Mañas. 2016. "Skeletal Muscle Regulates Metabolism via Interorgan Crosstalk: Roles in Health and Disease." *Journal of the American Medical Directors Association* 17 (9): 789–96. https://doi .org/10.1016/j.jamda.2016.04.019.

11. Nimmo, M. A., M. Leggate, J. L. Viana, and J. A. King. 2013. "The Effect of Physical Activity on Mediators of Inflammation." *Diabetes, Obesity and Metabolism* 15 (s3): 51–60. https://doi.org/10.1111/dom.12156.

12. Agudelo, Leandro Z., Teresa Femenía, Funda Orhan, Margareta Porsmyr-Palmertz, Michel Goiny, Vicente Martinez-Redondo, Jorge C. Correia, et al. 2014. "Skeletal Muscle PGC-1α1 Modulates Kynurenine Metabolism and Mediates Resilience to Stress-Induced Depression." *Cell* 159 (1): 33–45. https://doi.org/10.1016/j.cell.2014.07.051.

13. Pedersen, Bente K. 2011. "Exercise-Induced Myokines and Their Role in Chronic Diseases." *Brain, Behavior, and Immunity*, Special Issue: Adaptive Immunity in the Central Nervous System Function, 25 (5): 811–16. https://doi.org/10.1016/j.bbi.2011.02.010.

14. Rothman, S. M., and M. P. Mattson. 2013. "Activity-Dependent, Stress-Responsive BDNF Signaling and the Quest for Optimal Brain Health and Resilience Throughout the Lifespan." *Neuroscience*, Steroid hormone actions in the CNS: the role of brain-derived neurotrophic factor (BDNF), 239 (June): 228–40. https://doi.org/10.1016/j.neuroscience.2012.10.014; Cotman, Carl W., and Nicole C. Berchtold. 2002. "Exercise: A Behavioral Intervention to Enhance Brain Health and Plasticity." *Trends in Neurosciences* 25 (6): 295–301. https://doi.org/10.1016/S0166-2236(02)02143-4.

15. O'Connor, Patrick J., Matthew P. Herring, and Amanda Caravalho. 2010. "Mental Health Benefits of Strength Training in Adults." *American Journal of Lifestyle Medicine* 4 (5): 377–96. https://doi.org/10.1177/1559827610368771.

16. Richardson, Thomas, Peter Elliott, and Ronald Roberts. 2013. "The Relationship Between Personal Unsecured Debt and Mental and Physical Health: A Systematic Review and Meta-Analysis." *Clinical Psychology Review* 33 (8): 1148–62. https://doi.org/10.1016/j.cpr.2013.08.009.

17. Hoeve, Machteld, Geert Jan J. M. Stams, Marion van der Zouwen, Margaretha Vergeer, Kitty Jurrius, and Jessica J. Asscher. 2014. "A Systematic Review of Financial Debt in Adolescents and Young Adults: Prevalence, Correlates and Associations with Crime." *PLOS ONE* 9 (8): e104909. https://doi.org/10.1371/journal.pone.0104909.

18. "The Neuropeptide Oxytocin Modulates Consumer Brand Relationships | Scientific Reports." n.d. Accessed June 15, 2020. https://www.nature.com/articles/srep14960.

19. Ainsworth, Ben, Rachael Eddershaw, Daniel Meron, David S. Baldwin, and Matthew Garner. 2013. "The Effect of Focused Attention and Open Monitoring Meditation on Attention Network Function in Healthy Volunteers." *Psychiatry Research* 210 (3): 1226–31. https://doi.org/10.1016/j.psychres.2013.09.002.

20. Valentine, Elizabeth R., and Philip L. G. Sweet. 1999. "Meditation and Attention: A Comparison of the Effects of Concentrative and Mindfulness Meditation on Sustained Attention." *Mental Health, Religion & Culture* 2 (1): 59–70. https://doi.org/10.1080/13674679908406332.

21. Hölzel, Britta K., James Carmody, Mark Vangel, Christina Congleton, Sita M. Yerramsetti, Tim Gard, and Sara W. Lazar. 2011. "Mindfulness Practice Leads to Increases in Regional Brain Gray Matter Density." *Psychiatry Research: Neuroimaging* 191 (1): 36–43. https://doi.org/10.1016/j.pscy-

chresns.2010.08.006; Luders, Eileen, Arthur W. Toga, Natasha Lepore, and Christian Gaser. 2009. "The Underlying Anatomical Correlates of Long-Term Meditation: Larger Hippocampal and Frontal Volumes of Gray Matter." *NeuroImage* 45 (3): 672–78. https://doi.org/10.1016/j.neuroimage .2008.12.061.

22. Hölzel, Britta K., Elizabeth A. Hoge, Douglas N. Greve, Tim Gard, J. David Creswell, Kirk Warren Brown, Lisa Feldman Barrett, Carl Schwartz, Dieter Vaitl, and Sara W. Lazar. 2013. "Neural Mechanisms of Symptom Improvements in Generalized Anxiety Disorder Following Mindfulness Training." *NeuroImage: Clinical* 2 (January): 448–58. https://doi.org/10.1016/j .nicl.2013.03.011.

23. Feldman, Greg, Jeff Greeson, and Joanna Senville. 2010. "Differential Effects of Mindful Breathing, Progressive Muscle Relaxation, and Loving-Kindness Meditation on Decentering and Negative Reactions to Repetitive Thoughts." *Behaviour Research and Therapy* 48 (10): 1002–11. https:// doi.org/10.1016/j.brat.2010.06.006.

24. Gotink, Rinske A., Meike W. Vernooij, M. Arfan Ikram, Wiro J. Niessen, Gabriel P. Krestin, Albert Hofman, Henning Tiemeier, and M. G. Myriam Hunink. 2018. "Meditation and Yoga Practice Are Associated With Smaller Right Amygdala Volume: The Rotterdam Study." *Brain Imaging and Behavior* 12 (6): 1631–39. https://doi.org/10.1007/s11682-018-9826-z.

25. Gotink, Rinske A., Rozanna Meijboom, Meike W. Vernooij, Marion Smits, and M. G. Myriam Hunink. 2016. "8-Week Mindfulness Based Stress Reduction Induces Brain Changes Similar to Traditional Long-Term Meditation Practice – A Systematic Review." *Brain and Cognition* 108 (October): 32–41. https://doi.org/10.1016/j.bandc.2016.07.001.

26. Tang, Yi-Yuan, Britta K. Hölzel, and Michael I. Posner. 2015. "The Neuroscience of Mindfulness Meditation." *Nature Reviews Neuroscience* 16 (4): 213–25. https://doi.org/10.1038/nrn3916; "Frontiers | Effects of Mindful-Attention and Compassion Meditation Training on Amygdala Response to Emotional Stimuli in an Ordinary, Non-Meditative State | Human Neuroscience." n.d. Accessed July 9, 2020. https://www.frontiersin .org/articles/10.3389/fnhum.2012.00292/full?source=post_page -----efb608794707----------------------.

27. Brewer, J. A., P. D. Worhunsky, J. R. Gray, Y.-Y. Tang, J. Weber, and H. Kober. 2011. "Meditation Experience Is Associated With Differences in Default Mode Network Activity and Connectivity." *Proceedings of the National Academy of Sciences* 108 (50): 20254–59. https://doi.org/10.1073 /pnas.1112029108.

28. Strine, Tara W., and Daniel P. Chapman. 2005. "Associations of Frequent Sleep Insufficiency With Health-Related Quality of Life and Health Behaviors." *Sleep Medicine* 6 (1): 23–27. https://doi.org/10.1016/j .sleep.2004.06.003.

29. Liu, Yong, Anne G. Wheaton, Daniel P. Chapman, Timothy J. Cunningham, Hua Lu, and Janet B. Croft. 2016. "Prevalence of Healthy Sleep Duration Among Adults—United States, 2014." *MMWR. Morbidity and Mortality Weekly Report* 65 (6): 137–41. https://doi.org/10.15585/mmwr.mm6506a1.

30. Ohayon, Maurice M. 2011. "Epidemiological Overview of Sleep Disorders in the General Population." *Sleep Medicine Research* 2 (1): 1–9. https://doi .org/10.17241/smr.2011.2.1.1.

31. Taheri, Shahrad, Ling Lin, Diane Austin, Terry Young, and Emmanuel Mignot. 2004. "Short Sleep Duration Is Associated With Reduced Leptin, Elevated Ghrelin, and Increased Body Mass Index." Edited by Philippe Froguel. *PLoS Medicine* 1 (3): e62. https://doi.org/10.1371/journal .pmed.0010062.

32. Edwards, Robert R., David M. Almeida, Brendan Klick, Jennifer A. Haythornthwaite, and Michael T. Smith. 2008. "Duration of Sleep Contributes to Next-Day Pain Report in the General Population." *PAIN®* 137 (1): 202–7. https://doi.org/10.1016/j.pain.2008.01.025.

33. Walker, Matthew. 2018. *Why We Sleep: Unlocking the Power of Sleep and Dreams*. New York: Scribner's.

34. Durmer, Jeffrey S., and David F. Dinges. 2005. "Neurocognitive Consequences of Sleep Deprivation." *Seminars in Neurology* 25 (1): 117–29. https://doi.org/10.1055/s-2005-867080.

35. Milner, Catherine E., and Kimberly A. Cote. 2009. "Benefits of Napping in Healthy Adults: Impact of Nap Length, Time of Day, Age, and Experience With Napping." *Journal of Sleep Research* 18 (2): 272–81. https://doi .org/10.1111/j.1365-2869.2008.00718.x.

36. Evans, Frederick J., Mary R. Cook, Harvey D. Cohen, Emily Carota Orne, and Martin T. Orne, 1977. "Appetitive and Replacement Naps: EEG and Behavior." 1977. https://www.sas.upenn.edu/psych/history/orne /evansetal1977science687689.html.

37. Barnes, Christopher M., and David T. Wagner. 2009. "Changing to Daylight Saving Time Cuts Into Sleep and Increases Workplace Injuries." *Journal of Applied Psychology* 94 (5): 1305–17. https://doi.org/10.1037/a0015320.

38. Valdez, Pablo, Candelaria Ramírez, and Aída García. 2003. "Adjustment of the Sleep-Wake Cycle to Small (1-2h) Changes in Schedule." *Biological Rhythm Research* 34 (2): 145–55. https://doi.org/10.1076 /brhm.34.2.145.14494.

39. Carletto, Sara, Thomas Borsato, and Marco Pagani. 2017. "The Role of Slow Wave Sleep in Memory Pathophysiology: Focus on Post-Traumatic Stress Disorder and Eye Movement Desensitization and Reprocessing." *Frontiers in Psychology* 8. https://doi.org/10.3389/fpsyg.2017.02050.

40. Astell-Burt, Thomas, Xiaoqi Feng, and Gregory S. Kolt. 2013. "Does Access to Neighbourhood Green Space Promote a Healthy Duration of Sleep? Novel Findings From a Cross-Sectional Study of 259 319 Australians." *BMJ Open* 3 (8): e003094. https://doi.org/10.1136/bmjopen-2013-003094.

41. Grigsby-Toussaint, Diana S., Kedir N. Turi, Mark Krupa, Natasha J. Williams, Seithikurippu R. Pandi-Perumal, and Girardin Jean-Louis. 2015. "Sleep Insufficiency and the Natural Environment: Results From the US Behavioral Risk Factor Surveillance System Survey." *Preventive Medicine* 78 (September): 78–84. https://doi.org/10.1016/j.ypmed.2015.07.011.

42. Morita, Emi, Makoto Imai, Masako Okawa, Tomiyasu Miyaura, and Soichiro Miyazaki. 2011. "A Before and After Comparison of the Effects of Forest Walking on the Sleep of a Community-Based Sample of People With Sleep Complaints." *BioPsychoSocial Medicine* 5 (1): 13. https://doi .org/10.1186/1751-0759-5-13.

43. Gong, Hong, Chen-Xu Ni, Yun-Zi Liu, Yi Zhang, Wen-Jun Su, Yong-Jie Lian, Wei Peng, and Chun-Lei Jiang. 2016. "Mindfulness Meditation for Insomnia: A Meta-Analysis of Randomized Controlled Trials." *Journal of*

Psychosomatic Research 89 (October): 1–6. https://doi.org/10.1016/j
.jpsychores.2016.07.016; Rusch, Heather L., Michael Rosario, Lisa M.
Levison, Anlys Olivera, Whitney S. Livingston, Tianxia Wu, and Jessica
M. Gill. 2019. "The Effect of Mindfulness Meditation on Sleep Quality: A
Systematic Review and Meta-Analysis of Randomized Controlled Trials."
Annals of the New York Academy of Sciences 1445 (1): 5–16. https://doi
.org/10.1111/nyas.13996.

44. Chennaoui, Mounir, Pierrick J. Arnal, Fabien Sauvet, and Damien Léger.
2015. "Sleep and Exercise: A Reciprocal Issue?" *Sleep Medicine Reviews* 20
(April): 59–72. https://doi.org/10.1016/j.smrv.2014.06.008.

45. Buman, Matthew P., Barbara A. Phillips, Shawn D. Youngstedt, Christopher
E. Kline, and Max Hirshkowitz. 2014. "Does Nighttime Exercise Really
Disturb Sleep? Results From the 2013 National Sleep Foundation Sleep in
America Poll." *Sleep Medicine* 15 (7): 755–61. https://doi.org/10.1016/j
.sleep.2014.01.008.

46. Haroon, Ebrahim, Charles L. Raison, and Andrew H. Miller. 2012. "Psycho-
neuroimmunology Meets Neuropsychopharmacology: Translational Implications of the Impact of Inflammation on Behavior." *Neuropsychopharmacology*
37 (1): 137–62. https://doi.org/10.1038/npp.2011.205.

47. "World Urbanization Prospects - Population Division - United Nations."
n.d. Accessed June 1, 2020. https://population.un.org/wup/.

48. Defined by the authors as "Physical health, Mental health, Spirituality,
Certainty and sense of control and security, Learning/capability, Inspiration/
fulfillment of imagination, Sense of place, Identity/autonomy, Connected-
ness/belonging, Subjective (overall) well-being."

49. Russell, Roly, Anne D. Guerry, Patricia Balvanera, Rachelle K. Gould, Xavier
Basurto, Kai M.A. Chan, Sarah Klain, Jordan Levine, and Jordan Tam.
2013. "Humans and Nature: How Knowing and Experiencing Nature Affect
Well-Being." *Annual Review of Environment and Resources* 38 (1): 473–502.
https://doi.org/10.1146/annurev-environ-012312-110838.

50. White, Mathew P., Ian Alcock, James Grellier, Benedict W. Wheeler, Terry
Hartig, Sara L. Warber, Angie Bone, Michael H. Depledge, and Lora E.
Fleming. 2019. "Spending at Least 120 Minutes a Week in Nature Is Associated With Good Health and Wellbeing." *Scientific Reports* 9 (1): 1–11.
https://doi.org/10.1038/s41598-019-44097-3.

51. Thompson Coon, J., K. Boddy, K. Stein, R. Whear, J. Barton, and M. H.
Depledge. 2011. "Does Participating in Physical Activity in Outdoor Natural
Environments Have a Greater Effect on Physical and Mental Wellbeing
Than Physical Activity Indoors? A Systematic Review." *Environmental Sci-
ence & Technology* 45 (5): 1761–72. https://doi.org/10.1021/es102947t.

52. Stigsdotter, Ulrika K., Ola Ekholm, Jasper Schipperijn, Mette Toftager, Finn
Kamper-Jørgensen, and Thomas B. Randrup. 2010. "Health Promoting
Outdoor Environments - Associations Between Green Space, and Health,
Health-Related Quality of Life and Stress Based on a Danish National Rep-
resentative Survey." *Scandinavian Journal of Public Health* 38 (4): 411–17.
https://doi.org/10.1177/1403494810367468.

53. Berg, Agnes E. van den, Jolanda Maas, Robert A. Verheij, and Peter P. Groenewegen. 2010. "Green Space as a Buffer Between Stressful Life Events
and Health." *Social Science & Medicine* 70 (8): 1203–10. https://doi

.org/10.1016/j.socscimed.2010.01.002; Maas, J., R. A. Verheij, S. de Vries, P. Spreeuwenberg, F. G. Schellevis, and P. P. Groenewegen. 2009. "Morbidity Is Related to a Green Living Environment." *Journal of Epidemiology & Community Health* 63 (12): 967–73. https://doi.org/10.1136/jech.2008 .079038.

54. Fan, Yingling, Kirti V. Das, and Qian Chen. 2011. "Neighborhood Green, Social Support, Physical Activity, and Stress: Assessing the Cumulative Impact." *Health & Place* 17 (6): 1202–11. https://doi.org/10.1016/j.healthplace .2011.08.008.

55. Mitchell, Richard, and Frank Popham. 2008. "Effect of Exposure to Natural Environment on Health Inequalities: An Observational Population Study." *Lancet* 372 (9650): 1655–60. https://doi.org/10.1016/S0140 -6736(08)61689-X.

56. Berto, Rita. 2014. "The Role of Nature in Coping With Psycho-Physiological Stress: A Literature Review on Restorativeness." *Behavioral Sciences* 4 (4): 394–409. https://doi.org/10.3390/bs4040394.

57. Ward Thompson, Catharine, Jenny Roe, Peter Aspinall, Richard Mitchell, Angela Clow, and David Miller. 2012. "More Green Space Is Linked to Less Stress in Deprived Communities: Evidence From Salivary Cortisol Patterns." *Landscape and Urban Planning* 105 (3): 221–29. https://doi .org/10.1016/j.landurbplan.2011.12.015.

58. Bratman, Gregory N., Gretchen C. Daily, Benjamin J. Levy, and James J. Gross. 2015. "The Benefits of Nature Experience: Improved Affect and Cognition." *Landscape and Urban Planning* 138 (June): 41–50. https://doi .org/10.1016/j.landurbplan.2015.02.005.

59. Pretty, Jules, Murray Griffin, Martin Sellens, and Chris Pretty. n.d. "Green Exercise: Complementary Roles of Nature, Exercise and Diet in Physical and Emotional Well-Being and Implications for Public Health Policy," 39.

60. "Brief Walks in Outdoor and Laboratory Environments: Effects on Affective Responses, Enjoyment, and Intentions to Walk for Exercise: Research Quarterly for Exercise and Sport." Vol 80, No 3. n.d. Accessed May 29, 2020. https://www.tandfonline.com/doi/abs/10.1080/02701367.2009 .10599600.

61. Ceci, Ruggero, and Peter Hassmén. 1991. "Self-Monitored Exercise at Three Different RPE Intensities in Treadmill vs Field Running." *Medicine & Science in Sports & Exercise* 23 (6): 732–38. https://doi .org/10.1249/00005768-199106000-00013.

62. "The Effects of Sensory Deprivation and Music on Perceived Exertion and Affect During Exercise." *Journal of Sport and Exercise Psychology* Volume 12 Issue 2 (1990). n.d. Accessed May 29, 2020. https://journals.humankinetics .com/view/journals/jsep/12/2/article-p167.xml.

63. Antonelli, Michele, Grazia Barbieri, and Davide Donelli. 2019. "Effects of Forest Bathing (Shinrin-Yoku) on Levels of Cortisol as a Stress Biomarker: A Systematic Review and Meta-Analysis." *International Journal of Biometeorology* 63 (8): 1117–34. https://doi.org/10.1007/s00484-019-01717-x.

64. Park, Bum Jin, Yuko Tsunetsugu, Tamami Kasetani, Takahide Kagawa, and Yoshifumi Miyazaki. 2009. "The Physiological Effects of Shinrin-Yoku (Taking in the Forest Atmosphere or Forest Bathing): Evidence from Field Experiments in 24 Forests Across Japan." *Environmental Health and Preven-*

tive Medicine 15 (1): 18. https://doi.org/10.1007/s12199-009-0086-9.
65. Li, Qing. 2010. "Effect of Forest Bathing Trips on Human Immune Function." *Environmental Health and Preventive Medicine* 15 (1): 9–17. https://doi.org/10.1007/s12199-008-0068-3.
66. Takano, T., K. Nakamura, and M. Watanabe. 2002. "Urban Residential Environments and Senior Citizens' Longevity in Megacity Areas: The Importance of Walkable Green Spaces." *Journal of Epidemiology and Community Health* 56 (12): 913–18. https://doi.org/10.1136/jech.56.12.913.
67. Grahn, Patrik, and Ulrika A. Stigsdotter. 2003. "Landscape Planning and Stress." *Urban Forestry & Urban Greening* 2 (1): 1–18. https://doi.org/10.1078/1618-8667-00019.
68. Sjerp de Vries, Robert A Verheij, Peter P Groenewegen, Peter Spreeuwenberg, 2003." n.d. "Natural Environments—Healthy Environments? An Exploratory Analysis of the Relationship Between Greenspace and Health." Accessed May 29, 2020. https://journals.sagepub.com/doi/abs/10.1068/a35111.
69. Field, Tiffany. 2010. "Touch for Socioemotional and Physical Well-Being: A Review." *Developmental Review* 30 (4): 367–83. https://doi.org/10.1016/j.dr.2011.01.001.
70. Xiong, X. J., S. J. Li, and Y. Q. Zhang. 2015. "Massage Therapy for Essential Hypertension: A Systematic Review." *Journal of Human Hypertension* 29 (3): 143–51. https://doi.org/10.1038/jhh.2014.52; Nelson, Nicole L. 2015. "Massage Therapy: Understanding the Mechanisms of Action on Blood Pressure. A Scoping Review." *Journal of the American Society of Hypertension* 9 (10): 785–93. https://doi.org/10.1016/j.jash.2015.07.009.
71. Feldman, Ruth, Magi Singer, and Orna Zagoory. 2010. "Touch Attenuates Infants' Physiological Reactivity to Stress." *Developmental Science* 13 (2): 271–78. https://doi.org/10.1111/j.1467-7687.2009.00890.x.
72. Morrison, India. 2016. "Keep Calm and Cuddle on: Social Touch as a Stress Buffer." *Adaptive Human Behavior and Physiology* 2 (4): 344–62. https://doi.org/10.1007/s40750-016-0052-x.
73. Tabatabaee, Amir, Mansoureh Tafreshi, Maryam Rassouli, Seyed Aledavood, Hamid Majd, and Farahmand. 2016. "Effect of Therapeutic Touch in Patients With Cancer: A Literature Review." *Medical Archives* 70 (2): 142. https://doi.org/10.5455/medarh.2016.70.142-147.
74. Linnemann, Alexandra, Beate Ditzen, Jana Strahler, Johanna M. Doerr, and Urs M. Nater. 2015. "Music Listening as a Means of Stress Reduction in Daily Life." *Psychoneuroendocrinology* 60 (October): 82–90. https://doi.org/10.1016/j.psyneuen.2015.06.008.
75. Baltazar, Margarida, Daniel Västfjäll, Erkin Asutay, Lina Koppel, and Suvi Saarikallio. 2019. "Is It Me or the Music? Stress Reduction and the Role of Regulation Strategies and Music." *Music & Science* 2 (January): 2059204319844161. https://doi.org/10.1177/2059204319844161.
76. Vivaldi's *Miserere*.
77. Thoma, Myriam V., Roberto La Marca, Rebecca Brönnimann, Linda Finkel, Ulrike Ehlert, and Urs M. Nater. 2013. "The Effect of Music on the Human Stress Response." *PLOS ONE* 8 (8): e70156. https://doi.org/10.1371/journal.pone.0070156.
78. Pachelbel's Canon in D major.

79. Knight, Wendy E. J., and Nikki S. Rickard. 2001. "Relaxing Music Prevents Stress-Induced Increases in Subjective Anxiety, Systolic Blood Pressure, and Heart Rate in Healthy Males and Females." *Journal of Music Therapy* 38 (4): 254–72. https://doi.org/10.1093/jmt/38.4.254.

80. Linnemann, Alexandra, Anna Schnersch, and Urs M. Nater. 2017. "Testing the Beneficial Effects of Singing in a Choir on Mood and Stress in a Longitudinal Study: The Role of Social Contacts." *Musicae Scientiae* 21 (2): 195–212. https://doi.org/10.1177/1029864917693295.

81. Keeler, Jason R. Edward A. Roth, Brittany L. Neuser, John M. Spitsbergen, Daniel James Maxwell Waters, and John-Mary Vianney. 2015. "The Neurochemistry and Social Flow of Singing: Bonding and Oxytocin." *Frontiers in Human Neuroscience* 9. https://doi.org/10.3389/fnhum.2015.00518.

82. Perkins, Rosie, Sara Ascenso, Louise Atkins, Daisy Fancourt, and Aaron Williamon. 2016. "Making Music for Mental Health: How Group Drumming Mediates Recovery." *Psychology of Well-Being* 6 (1): 11. https://doi.org/10.1186/s13612-016-0048-0.

83. Martin, Karen Emma, and Lisa Jane Wood. 2017. "Drumming to a New Beat: A Group Therapeutic Drumming and Talking Intervention to Improve Mental Health and Behaviour of Disadvantaged Adolescent Boys." *Children Australia* 42 (4): 268–76. https://doi.org/10.1017/cha.2017.40; Suh, Eun. 2015. "The Use of Therapeutic Group Drumming With Korean Middle School Students in School Violence Prevention Programs." *Expressive Therapies Dissertations*, November. https://digitalcommons.lesley.edu/expressive_dissertations/64.

84. Newman, Garth F., Clint Maggott, and Debbie G. Alexander. 2015. "Group Drumming as a Burnout Prevention Initiative Among Staff Members at a Child and Adolescent Mental Health Care Facility." *South African Journal of Psychology* 45 (4): 439–51. https://doi.org/10.1177/0081246315581346.

85. Sarah C. Slayton MA, ATR-BC, ATR-BC Jeanne D'Archer MA, and ATR-BC Frances Kaplan DA. 2010. "Outcome Studies on the Efficacy of Art Therapy: A Review of Findings." *Art Therapy* 27 (3): 108–18. https://doi.org/10.1080/07421656.2010.10129660.

CHAPTER 5

1. Holt-Lunstad, Julianne, Timothy B. Smith, and J. Bradley Layton. 2010. "Social Relationships and Mortality Risk: A Meta-Analytic Review." *PLOS Medicine* 7 (7): e1000316. https://doi.org/10.1371/journal.pmed.1000316.

2. Uchino, Bert N. 2009. "Understanding the Links Between Social Support and Physical Health: A Life-Span Perspective With Emphasis on the Separability of Perceived and Received Support." *Perspectives on Psychological Science* 4 (3): 236–55. https://doi.org/10.1111/j.1745-6924.2009.01122.x.

3. Heinrichs, Markus, Thomas Baumgartner, Clemens Kirschbaum, and Ulrike Ehlert. 2003. "Social Support and Oxytocin Interact to Suppress Cortisol and Subjective Responses to Psychosocial Stress." *Biological Psychiatry* 54 (12): 1389–98. https://doi.org/10.1016/s0006-3223(03)00465-7.

4. Cosley, Brandon J., Shannon K. McCoy, Laura R. Saslow, and Elissa S. Epel. 2010. "Is Compassion for Others Stress Buffering? Consequences

of Compassion and Social Support for Physiological Reactivity to Stress." *Journal of Experimental Social Psychology* 46 (5): 816–23. https://doi .org/10.1016/j.jesp.2010.04.008.

5. Miller, Jonas G., Sarah Kahle, Monica Lopez, and Paul D. Hastings. 2015. "Compassionate Love Buffers Stress-Reactive Mothers From Fight-or-Flight Parenting." *Developmental Psychology* 51 (1): 36–43. https://doi.org/10.1037 /a0038236.

6. Bluth, Karen, Patricia N. E. Roberson, Susan A. Gaylord, Keturah R. Faurot, Karen M. Grewen, Samantha Arzon, and Susan S. Girdler. 2016. "Does Self-Compassion Protect Adolescents From Stress?" *Journal of Child and Family Studies* 25 (4): 1098–1109. https://doi.org/10.1007/s10826-015 -0307-3.

7. Hu, Yueqin, Yuyin Wang, Yifang Sun, Javier Arteta-Garcia, and Stephanie Purol. 2018. "Diary Study: The Protective Role of Self-Compassion on Stress-Related Poor Sleep Quality." *Mindfulness* 9 (6): 1931–40. https://doi .org/10.1007/s12671-018-0939-7.

8. Kaurin, Aleksandra, Sandra Schönfelder, and Michèle Wessa. 2018. "Self-Compassion Buffers the Link Between Self-Criticism and Depression in Trauma-Exposed Firefighters." *Journal of Counseling Psychology* 65 (4): 453–62. https://doi.org/10.1037/cou0000275.

9. Kaurin, Aleksandra, Sandra Schönfelder, and Michèle Wessa. 2018. "Self-Compassion Buffers the Link Between Self-Criticism and Depression in Trauma-Exposed Firefighters." *Journal of Counseling Psychology* 65 (4): 453–62. https://doi.org/10.1037/cou0000275.

10. Mascaro, Jennifer S., Sean Kelley, Alana Darcher, Lobsang Tenzin Negi, Carol Worthman, Andrew Miller, and Charles Raison. 2018. "Meditation Buffers Medical Student Compassion From the Deleterious Effects of Depression." *Journal of Positive Psychology* 13 (2): 133–42. https://doi.org/10 .1080/17439760.2016.1233348.

11. Delaney, Martin C. 2018. "Caring for the Caregivers: Evaluation of the Effect of an Eight-Week Pilot Mindful Self-Compassion (MSC) Training Program on Nurses' Compassion Fatigue and Resilience." *PLOS ONE* 13 (11): e0207261. https://doi.org/10.1371/journal.pone.0207261.

12. Eldor, Liat. 2018. "Public Service Sector: The Compassionate Workplace— The Effect of Compassion and Stress on Employee Engagement, Burnout, and Performance." *Journal of Public Administration Research and Theory* 28 (1): 86–103. https://doi.org/10.1093/jopart/mux028.

13. Zimet, Gregory D., Nancy W. Dahlem, Sara G. Zimet, and Gordon K. Farley. 1988. "The Multidimensional Scale of Perceived Social Support." *Journal of Personality Assessment* 52 (1): 30–41. https://doi.org/10.1207 /s15327752jpa5201_2.

14. The phrase "social support" often has a broader definition, encompassing physical and spiritual support from others.

15. Piferi, Rachel L., and Kathleen A. Lawler. 2006. "Social Support and Ambulatory Blood Pressure: An Examination of Both Receiving and Giving." *International Journal of Psychophysiology* 62 (2): 328–36. https://doi.org/10.1016/j .ijpsycho.2006.06.002; Sneed, Rodlescia S., and Sheldon Cohen. 2013. "A Prospective Study of Volunteerism and Hypertension Risk in Older Adults." *Psychology and Aging* 28 (2): 578–86. https://doi.org/10.1037/a0032718.

16. MarYam G. Hamedani, Hazel Rose Markus, Alyssa S. Fu, 2011." n.d.

"My Nation, My Self: Divergent Framings of America Influence American Selves." Accessed June 16, 2020. https://journals.sagepub.com/doi/abs /10.1177/0146167211398139.

17. Nahum-Shani, Inbal, Peter Bamberger, and Samuel Bacharach. 2011. "Social Support and Employee Well-Being: The Conditioning Effect of Perceived Patterns of Supportive Exchange." *Journal of Health and Social Behavior* 52 (March): 123–39. https://doi.org/10.1177/0022146510395024.

18. "Curiosity: Our Superpower for Everything From Breaking Bad Habits to Overcoming Anxiety." 2020. *Dr. Jud* (blog). March 9, 2020. https://drjud .com/curiosity-superpower/.

19. Scott, Susan. 2004. *Fierce Conversations: Achieving Success at Work & in Life, One Conversation at a Time.* Penguin.

20. Cardoso, Christopher, Christopher Kalogeropoulos, Christopher A. Brown, Mark Anthony Orlando, and Mark A. Ellenbogen. 2016. "Memory Response to Oxytocin Predicts Relationship Dissolution Over 18 Months." *Psychoneuroendocrinology* 68 (June): 171–76. https://doi.org/10.1016/j.psyneuen .2016.03.005.

21. Calhoun, Lawrence G., and Richard G. Tedeschi. 2004. "AUTHORS' RESPONSE: 'The Foundations of Posttraumatic Growth: New Considerations.'" *Psychological Inquiry* 15 (1): 93–102. https://doi.org/10.1207 /s15327965pli1501_03.

22. Matthew D. Lieberman, Naomi I. Eisenberger, Molly J. Crockett, Sabrina M. Tom, Jennifer H. Pfeifer, Baldwin M. Way, 2007." n.d. "Putting Feelings Into Words." Accessed July 9, 2020. https://journals.sagepub.com/doi /abs/10.1111/j.1467-9280.2007.01916.x.

23. Streamer, L., Seery, M. D., Kondrak, C. L., Lamarche, V. M., & Saltsman, T. L. (2017). "Not I, But She: The beneficial effects of Self-distancing on Challenge/Threat Cardiovascular Responses." *Journal of Experimental Social Psychology* 70, 235–241. https://doi.org/10.1016/j.jesp.2016.11.008.

24. This is not something you should attempt to lead without training.

25. To respect confidentiality, I'll only say that I learned this from people on Steve's senior management team at NeXT, who were startled when Steve offered to reach out to John Sculley, the Apple chair who fired him.

26. Lumma, Anna-Lena, Bethany E. Kok, and Tania Singer. 2015. "Is Meditation Always Relaxing? Investigating Heart Rate, Heart Rate Variability, Experienced Effort and Likeability During Training of Three Types of Meditation." *International Journal of Psychophysiology* 97 (1): 38–45. https:// doi.org/10.1016/j.ijpsycho.2015.04.017.

27. Hofmann, Stefan G., Paul Grossman, and Devon E. Hinton. 2011. "Loving-Kindness and Compassion Meditation: Potential for Psychological Interventions." *Clinical Psychology Review* 31 (7): 1126–32. https://doi .org/10.1016/j.cpr.2011.07.003.

28. Carson, James W., Francis J. Keefe, Thomas R. Lynch, Kimberly M. Carson, Veeraindar Goli, Anne Marie Fras, and Steven R. Thorp. 2005. "Loving-Kindness Meditation for Chronic Low Back Pain: Results From a Pilot Trial." *Journal of Holistic Nursing* 23 (3): 287–304. https://doi.org /10.1177/0898010105277651.

29. Hutcherson, Cendri A., Emma M. Seppala, and James J. Gross. 2008. "Loving-Kindness Meditation Increases Social Connectedness." *Emotion* 8 (5): 720–24. https://doi.org/10.1037/a0013237.

30. Neill, James T. "Challenge and Support in Outward Bound: The Double-Edged Sword," 7.

31. Phipps, Sean, Alanna Long, Victoria W. Willard, Yuko Okado, Melissa Hudson, Qinlei Huang, Hui Zhang, and Robert Noll. 2015. "Parents of Children With Cancer: At-Risk or Resilient?" *Journal of Pediatric Psychology* 40 (9): 914–25. https://doi.org/10.1093/jpepsy/jsv047.

32. For a fascinating, encouraging, and thorough exploration of this idea, read Matt Ridley's *The Rational Optimist*.

CHAPTER 6

1. Bronk, Kendall Cotton, Patrick L. Hill, Daniel K. Lapsley, Tasneem L. Talib, and Holmes Finch. 2009. "Purpose, Hope, and Life Satisfaction in Three Age Groups." *Journal of Positive Psychology* 4 (6): 500–510. https://doi.org/10.1080/17439760903271439.

2. Young, J. Scott, Craig S. Cashwell, and Julia Shcherbakova. 2000. "The Moderating Relationship of Spirituality on Negative Life Events and Psychological Adjustment." *Counseling and Values* 45 (1): 49–57. https://doi.org/10.1002/j.2161-007X.2000.tb00182.x.

3. Lê, Christine, Erik P. Ingvarson, and Richard C. Page. 1995. "Alcoholics Anonymous and the Counseling Profession: Philosophies in Conflict." *Journal of Counseling & Development* 73 (6): 603–9. https://doi.org/10.1002/j.1556-6676.1995.tb01803.x.

4. Park, Crystal, and Lawrence H. Cohen. 1992. "Religious Beliefs and Practices and the Coping Process." In *Personal Coping: Theory, Research, and Application*, 185–98. Westport, CT, US: Praeger Publishers/Greenwood Publishing Group; "Assessment and Prediction of Stress-Related Growth." Park—1996—Journal of Personality—Wiley Online Library." n.d. Accessed June 30, 2020. https://onlinelibrary.wiley.com/doi/abs/10.1111/j.1467-6494.1996.tb00815.x.

5. Cai, Denise J., Sarnoff A. Mednick, Elizabeth M. Harrison, Jennifer C. Kanady, and Sara C. Mednick. 2009. "REM, Not Incubation, Improves Creativity by Priming Associative Networks." *Proceedings of the National Academy of Sciences* 106 (25): 10130–34. https://doi.org/10.1073/pnas.0900271106.

6. Sherman, David, and Geoffrey Cohen. 2002. "Accepting Threatening Information: Self–Affirmation and the Reduction of Defensive Biases." *Current Directions in Psychological Science - CURR DIRECTIONS PSYCHOL SCI* 11 (August): 119–23. https://doi.org/10.1111/1467-8721.00182.

7. Koole, Sander L., Karianne Smeets, Ad van Knippenberg, and Ap Dijksterhuis. 1999. "The Cessation of Rumination Through Self-Affirmation." *Journal of Personality and Social Psychology* 77 (1): 111–25. https://doi.org/10.1037/0022-3514.77.1.111.

8. David A. K. Sherman, Leif D. Nelson, Claude M. Steele, 2000." n.d. "Do Messages About Health Risks Threaten the Self? Increasing the Acceptance of Threatening Health Messages Via Self-Affirmation." Accessed July 17, 2020. https://journals.sagepub.com/doi/abs/10.1177/01461672002611003.

9. Creswell, J. D., W. T. Welch, S. E. Taylor, D. K. Sherman, T. L. Grue-

newald, and T. Mann. 2005. "Affirmation of Personal Values Buffers Neuroendocrine and Psychological Stress Responses." *Psychological Science* 16 (11): 846–51. https://doi.org/10.1111/j.1467-9280.2005.01624.x.

10. As a consultant in the 1990s, I worked on technology plans for the White House, for the president's daily security briefing, which meant that I was familiar with the system of intelligence checks and balances that clearly were bypassed to create justifications for the Iraq war.

other resources

PHYSICAL

The Body Keeps the Score. Bessel van der Kolk, 2015.
When the Body Says No: Understanding the Stress-Disease Connection. Gabor Maté, 2011.
The Upside of Stress: Why Stress is Good for You, and How to Get Good at It. Kelly McGonigal, 2015.
Why We Sleep. Matthew Walker, 2017.

SOCIAL

The Lost Art of Good Conversation: A Mindful Way to Connect With Others and Enrich Everyday Life. Sakyong Mipham, 2017.
Fierce Conversations: Achieving Success at Work and in Life One Conversation at a Time. Susan Scott, 2004.
Trust After Trauma: A Guide to Relationships for Survivors and Those Who Love Them. Aphrodite T. Matsakis, 1998.
Give and Take: Why Helping Others Drives Our Success. Adam Grant, 2013.

SPIRITUAL

Forgive for Good. Frederic Luskin, 2003.
The Gifts of Imperfection: Let Go of Who You Think You're Supposed to Be and Embrace Who You Are. Brené Brown, 2010.
Connecting: A Radical New Vision. Larry Crabb, 1997.
Falling Upward. Richard Rohr, 2011.
Breathing Under Water. Richard Rohr, 2011.
Abba's Child: The Cry of the Heart for Intimate Belonging. Brennan Manning, 2015.

GENERAL

The Mayo Clinic Guide to Stress-Free Living. Amit Sood, 2013.
The Johns Hopkins Guide to Psychological First Aid, George S. Everly, Jr., Jeffrey M. Lating, 2017.

The Rational Optimist. Matt Ridley, 2011.

Resilient: How to Grow an Unshakable Core of Calm Strength and Happiness. Rick Hanson, 2018.

In the Realm of Hungry Ghosts. Gabor Maté, 2010.

Mindset: The New Psychology of Success. Carol S. Dweck, 2007.

EFT and Tapping for Beginners. Rockridge Press, 2013.

The Happiness Hypothesis: Finding Truth in Ancient Wisdom. Jonathan Haidt, 2006.

Happify

index

about the author

Nick Arnett is a wildland firefighter/EMT, crisis responder, fire chaplain, and former paramedic. He has experience in domestic and international emergency and disaster response in fire, rescue, medical, communications, public information, and crisis intervention roles. Arnett also teaches crisis intervention, resilience, and community emergency preparedness. He previously was a software industry product executive and company founder with seven patents for intelligence-gathering software methods.

Arnett has also been an award-winning reporter for radio, television, and print, including CBS and ABC News, *Rolling Stone*, and numerous technology publications. While at the *San Jose Business Journal*, he broke the story of Steve Jobs's departure from Apple. While in college, he reported the first accurate account of the Reagan shooting for CBS and other news media.

Arnett holds numerous certifications in emergency medicine, wildland firefighting, rescue, crisis intervention, and emergency management. He is also a General Class ham radio operator (KJ6FOI) active in emergency communications with CAL FIRE and ARES/RACES.